D1315046

101

Best Weekend

Businesses

By
Dan Ramsey

CAREER PRESS
3 Tice Road
P.O. Box 687
Franklin Lakes, NJ 07417
1-800-CAREER-1
201-848-0310 (NJ and outside U.S.)
FAX: 201-848-1727

101 BEST WEEKEND BUSINESSES

ISBN 1-56414-257-4, $14.99

Cover design by The Hub Graphics Corp.

Printed in the U.S.A. by Book-mart Press

To order this title by mail, please include price as noted above, $2.50 handling per order and $1.00 for each book ordered. Send to: Career Press, Inc., 3 Tice Road, P.O. Box 687, Franklin Lakes, NJ 07417.

Or call toll-free 1-800-CAREER-1 (NJ and Canada: 201-848-0310) to order using VISA or MasterCard, or for further information on books from Career Press.

Library of Congress Cataloging-in-Publication Data

Ramsey, Dan, 1945-
    101 best weekend businesses / by Dan Ramsey.
        p.   cm.
    Includes index.
    ISBN 1-56414-257-4 (paper)
    1. Home-based businesses--Management. 2. New business
enterprises--Management.   I. Title.
HD62.38.R36   1996
658'.041--dc20   96-35405
                                                                              CIP

To you, the reader. May God's blessings flow in your home and your business.

Acknowledgments

This book is produced by a home business: the Cottage Company. It has been a part-time business for 31 years and a full-time business for more than three years. The business has changed names three times, but the focus has always been about the same: helping others through information. Along the way, I've owned a variety of other businesses, as well as worked for many small business owners. I've learned from each situation. Even so, there was much more to learn from others.

Thanks to many people who contributed to the development of this book. They include Katie Goering of American Business Lists; Lori Capps and Roy L. Fietz of the Business Development Center at Southwest Oregon Community College; The Small Business Administration Office of Business Development; the Service Corps of Retired Executives; the U.S. Department of Commerce, Office of Business Liaison and Minority Business Development Agency; the U.S. Treasury; and the Internal Revenue Service. Special thanks go to Neil Soderstrom and to the staff of the Cottage Company.

Business forms in this book were produced using PerFORM Forms Designer for Windows from Delrina Technology Inc.

All brand and product names mentioned in this book are copyright, trademarks or registered trademarks/tradenames of their respective owners. Names, addresses, telephone numbers and related information are included in this book for the convenience of the reader and were current when this book was written. No endorsement is implied.

Contents

Part 1

Introduction

It's a quiet revolution. The National Association of Home-Based Businesses reports that there are now between 12 and 15 *million* home businesses in the United States. And the number grows daily. The largest group of these new entrepreneurs includes those who are tired of sharing the profits of their efforts with an employer. By need or desire, these men and women are reversing the industrial revolution that moved jobs from homes to factories. People are setting up their own cottage companies—part-time home-based businesses.

What kind of companies? You name it. These revolutionaries are offering products and services to a new world based on common needs, rather than common geography. The new businesses are using technology to reach out to a wider world. They are also focusing on the value of service. They are making a good living in or from their home.

So can you.

101 Best Weekend Businesses is a step-by-step guide to starting and running a successful home business on weekends and during other spare time—less than 20 hours a week—without a lot of startup cash. It will motivate you with examples of how others have succeeded with their home businesses. Most important, it offers more than 100 home-business possibilities—with specific information and resources for starting and operating each.

Part 1 of this book will help you decide if there is a part-time home business for you and, if so, how to get started. It will help you plan the success of your cottage company. It will guide you through the planning process to help ensure that you find the home business that best fits your goals. You'll consider what you'll be doing, what you need to start, your customers, pricing and profits.

Part 2 is big. It includes 101 types of weekend businesses that now offer millions of people a good income for their time and efforts.

Each profile includes concise answers to the six questions you'll consider in Chapter 2:

- ◆ What will I be doing?
- ◆ What will I need to start?
- ◆ Who will my customers be?
- ◆ How much should I charge?
- ◆ How much will I make?
- ◆ How can I get started?

At the end of this book are blank worksheets to help you analyze specific weekend and part-time opportunities, resources, potential customers, pricing and income and expenses. Additional forms help you track business income and expenses, manage inventory, invoice customers and make sure cash is flowing in the right direction.

Why am I writing this book? Because I love helping others reach their goals through home businesses. As president of Ramsey Business Strategies, a consulting service specializing in helping small businesses grow, and as a partner in the Cottage Company, a consulting service that develops startup plans for small home or cottage businesses, I've had a chance to help many small business owners. Now with this book, I hope I can help you too. I've written more than 25 books on small business opportunities. Each book has had the same purpose: to help others discover and reach their goals through knowledge and wisdom. And each book I've written has taught me more about how to do so as I interview and learn from others.

Chapter 1

Is there a weekend home business for you?

- "There's too much month left at the end of the money."
- "I need to make a living, but I also need to be home with my family."
- "I can't find a job in my town, and I can't afford to move."
- "I need a second income for a while to pay off an unexpected bill."
- "I don't want to commute three hours a day to a job I don't enjoy."

There are many practical reasons why you need or want to make money at home in your spare time. Whether you're a student or a retiree, whether you're feeling financially challenged or professionally unchallenged, you can often gain more of what you desire from life by working at home. There will be problems to overcome, however, and working at home will take some extra discipline.

First, let me explain what I mean by a "home business." We've all seen those ads in the back of magazines—"Send me 10 bucks and I'll show you how to make a million." (By having a hundred thousand people send you 10 bucks!) The problem is that stuffing envelopes or selling flavored tofu from home aren't really legitimate businesses. They're just a "secret" way for others to make money at home by selling information.

So how can you *legitimately* make money at home? I've made money at home for many years as a writer and a business consultant. I've guided thousands of others in selecting and building successful small businesses. What I've discovered is that there is no get-rich-quick path, no magical formula to home business success. It's hard work, but it can also be lots of fun.

Why start your business at home?

Usually, someone starting a home business sets up a small office at the dining table, in a walk-in closet, an extra bedroom or a workshop. This is an ideal situation for a part-time business for many reasons. First, there will be little or no additional rent expense. It is also convenient—there's no commute and you have all your records with you to review at any time. In addition, a family member or someone living with you can answer the telephone while you're away. And you can legally deduct some of your household costs as legitimate expenses and reduce your tax obligation.

But the best reason for a home office is that it saves you time. A client can call you in the evening to ask about a specific job and you can respond immediately without leaving your home.

Of course, with a home office you will want to discourage walk-in customers. Don't include your address in your ads. Rather, have prospects call you to set up appointments. Make sure the path from your front door to your office is short and looks as professional as possible.

Remember, though, operating a business from your home is usually only temporary and only for part-time businesses. Once you've developed a clientele and are ready to make your business full-time, seriously consider a commercial location.

The IRS says you can deduct part of your home expenses for business purposes. By a home, they mean a house, apartment, condominium, mobile home, boat, unattached garage, studio, barn or greenhouse. The IRS says that the physical portion of the home you deduct must be used exclusively and regularly in conducting business. It must be either the principal place of your business, a place where you regularly meet with customers or a separate structure used in connection with your trade. There are more specific definitions of "exclusive use," "regular use" and "principal place of business" in Publication 587.

What home business expenses can you deduct and which can you not? In many cases, you can deduct all expenses directly required by the business, no matter where it is located. For example, you can deduct the cost of a telephone used exclusively for business calls. In addition, you can deduct a percentage of your indirect housing expenses, depending on how much of your home is used for the business. Indirect expenses include mortgage interest, real estate taxes, insurance, utilities, depreciation and repairs.

How much you can deduct for the business use of your home depends on how much of your home is used for business. For example, if your home is 1,200 square feet in size and you use 300 square feet, or 25 percent, of it for your business, you will be able to deduct 25 percent of the indirect expenses of your home.

A word of warning: The home office expense is one of the most abused deductions in the tax system. The IRS carefully looks at tax filings that include this expense. Most are legitimate, but those who pad their home office expense deductions make it difficult for those who honestly use a portion of their home to conduct business.

Find the best weekend home business

What if you don't have much capital or many special skills? Is there a home business for you? Probably. You may have to search a little harder than the Nobel prize-winning-scientist-turned-consultant, but you can find a home business that fits you and your marketplace.

What type of home businesses are successful? Here are some rules of business I've learned:

Rule 1: Businesses that require large inventories of products cost too much to start and succeed. Find a business that serves others with service or low-cost products.

Rule 2: People don't buy things that don't give their lives value. You wouldn't buy a TV that didn't work or a book written in Greek (unless you can read Greek). Make sure your business offers your customers a value that is greater than the price they pay you.

Rule 3: Advertising costs money. Find a business that is so unique that people will tell others about it (word-of-mouth advertising). If it's not a unique business, find a way of making it unique. Add a unique benefit, a special service or a new approach to your business to make it easier to promote and to remember. Keep advertising costs to a minimum.

What I'm describing here is called a "cottage company." A cottage company is a home business that profits by adding value to the lives of others. (In fact, the name of one of my home businesses is The Cottage Company.) A cottage company can be operated from a house, apartment, duplex, condominium or other residential structure.

How can you decide which cottage company offers you the most satisfaction and profit? By considering your abilities and skills in three areas. Answer the following questions by rating yourself from 1 to 10 (1 is low, 10 is high):

Physical skills

___ Are you handy with your hands?
___ Have you made or repaired things?
___ Are you interested in how things work?
___ Are you artistic in any way?

Intellectual skills

___ Do you enjoy solving puzzles or riddles?
___ Do you easily remember and quote facts?
___ Do you have unique knowledge or training?
___ Do you have resources for specialized knowledge?

Social skills

___ Do you like meeting new people?
___ Do you enjoy talking with strangers?
___ Do you like helping others?
___ Do you like to analyze how people think or act?

Also rate yourself, 1 to 10, in motivation to start and run a home business. Are you willing to spend many hours planning and promoting your business before you see your first dollar? Is it a service that you will enjoy offering to others? Will you be proud to tell friends what you do?

Rating your skills and motivation in these areas can help you select a cottage company that will give you both personal income and personal satisfaction. It can tell you whether your cottage company should offer physical, intellectual or social skills—or all three to different degrees.

The following are some questions to help you determine what you enjoy doing.

♦ Is there anything that people often compliment you about? A talent, hobby, or skill?

♦ Is there some work or task you would do even if you weren't paid?

♦ Is there some cause or mission that drives you?

♦ Is there some opportunity that strikes you as worthwhile?

Chapter 2 will help you apply your skills and interests to a home business that you can enjoy.

What are you looking for?

Maybe by this stage in your life you've developed a list of personal goals for the next year, five years and beyond. Most people have not. It isn't mandatory that you develop a long list of your life's goals before you start a home business, but it will increase your chances of personal and financial success.

A *goal* is an objective. It is somewhere you want to be or something you want to have. It can be the goal of owning your own home business. Or it may be the option of working at home. Or it can be amassing $1 million in assets within 20 years to fund your retirement. Whatever they are, they are your personal goals and they reflect who you are and what you want from your life. Think about them. We'll discuss them further in the next chapter, but in the meantime, spend some time thinking about your goals.

There are three types of cottage companies, each reflecting a specific type of goal. These home business types are lifestyle businesses, income businesses and social businesses. Each of the businesses in this book can be approached as one these types of businesses, depending on your primary goals. They will typically combine all three elements, but one type is the main focus.

Lifestyle businesses

Lifestyle businesses try to refute the adage to never combine business with pleasure. Lifestyle businesses instead show that a pleasure can become a business and vice versa.

Let me give you some examples. For someone who enjoys dogs and cats, a pet-sitting business can be a real pleasure. For car enthusiasts, an auto detailing service that cleans and shines cars can make going to work fun. But the car enthusiast may dislike dogs and cats, so starting a pet-sitting business wouldn't be a lifestyle business.

What lifestyle businesses should you consider? All that capture your interest. The adage to "do what you love and the money will follow" is simplistic, but frequently true. Building a business around a passion can help you overcome any reluctance to sell. It can give you motivation to share your skills and profit from them.

Sometimes a lifestyle business isn't based on passion, but on your situation. You may choose a lifestyle business because of a disability or because of limited local employment opportunities. For example, when the major employer in a small town closed down, one man wanted to remain in the town and continue his volunteer work on the city council until retirement. He started a cottage company. In another example, a business was begun so a mother could be at home when her children were out of school. Some businesses are built to fit lifestyle goals.

Income businesses

An income business is one that focuses on bringing in a healthy profit for the owner. Doing what's fun is a secondary goal—or maybe not even a consideration. An income business is started and operated to produce the greatest income with the least expenses. Examples of income businesses include antique dealers, importers/exporters, business consultants and collection services. Though the business may be based on the owner's interests or passions, the primary purpose of the business is to be profitable.

Why do people consider income businesses over lifestyle businesses? For money, of course. The loss of a job, unplanned expenses or plans to build a nest egg are all good reasons for starting an income business at home.

For thousands of years, most home businesses were primarily income businesses. Farmers raised crops more to sell than to eat or because they enjoyed growing things. Cabinetmakers made cabinets to produce an income long after the enjoyment of woodworking expired.

Yes, you can combine income and pleasure in a business. However, the emphasis is typically on one or the other. So you must decide which is more important to your goals.

Social businesses

A social business is one that emphasizes helping others. Of course, any business that trades products or services for money must help others or the trade will never happen. However, some businesses emphasize social contacts over income or owner's lifestyle needs. These businesses can be considered paid volunteerism.

An Iowa housewife felt she was becoming too much of a homebody and yearned for contact with others. However, because she lived in the country away from employment opportunities, she decided to start and build a social home business. She started an income tax service, focusing on helping farmers keep records and pay taxes. She could have built the business primarily for income or as a lifestyle business, but she instead developed it as a way to meet and help her neighbors.

Other social businesses include bed-and-breakfasts, bridal consultants, care givers and companions to the elderly.

What do you know about yourself?

Starting a business, getting married and buying a house or a car are all big decisions that require some self-reflection. That's good. This gives you a chance to consider what you want and don't want, as well as what skills and ideas you have to offer. Let's look at some of the qualities and values that can help you succeed with your home business.

Self-awareness. The process of starting and operating any business is difficult. It will require that you constantly test yourself, maintaining what works and changing what doesn't. That's what many people love about being a business owner: the endless challenges. It makes them aware of their characteristics and requires that they continue to grow.

Hard work. As you start and grow your home business, you'll spend at least eight hours a day with your primary job (employee, homemaker, etc.), then another two to six hours with your home business. You must work hard to get ahead with a home business.

Discipline. Discipline is the power behind hard work. You can know exactly what needs to be done and still not do it. Self-discipline forces you to act. Having goals that are meaningful to you will increase your self-discipline.

Independence. Great business owners often make poor employees. They're too independent. They cannot, however, be stubborn. Business owners must maintain a balance between independence and open-mindedness to succeed.

Self-confidence. It takes a lot of nerve to start a business. It takes a lot more to make it successful. Nerve or self-confidence isn't the same as ego. It's a belief in your unique skills founded on past successes. You know you can successfully operate a home business because you have the skills to do so, not just the desire.

Adaptability. Life is chaos. No matter how much we plan, people and events change. Products change. Markets change. We change. A successful business owner must adapt to these changes. Without change, life becomes very dull.

Judgment. To succeed in business, you must make good decisions every day. Wisdom requires knowledge. You must be able to gather complete and accurate facts and make the best decision you can from those facts. You will not be right every time, but you will be right most of the time. This is good judgment.

Stress tolerance. Stress is defined as "the confusion created when one's mind overrides the body's basic desire to clobber some yo-yo who desperately deserves it." Humor can help reduce stress. Stress is a part of everyday life, especially in business. Learning to live with stress without taking it personally can help you succeed in business.

Need to achieve. Success is the achievement of something you go after. It may be the completion of a project, the start of a business or the learning of a new skill. This need is a driving force in successful business owners and helps give them the energy to reach their goal.

8 steps to starting your business

There are eight proven steps to starting and succeeding with a cottage company you've selected. Here they are:

Step 1. Know your business. Whatever business you select, you must know more about it than the people you serve with it. If the business is in a field that is new to you, learn as much as you can. For example, as an auto detailer you must learn about car paints, waxes, finishes and detailing equipment, as well as develop skills that make auto detailing efficient. How can you know your business? Work for or study your competitors. Buy their services and read their ads. Improve on what they do. Ask a librarian for information on trade associations and magazines that serve those in your selected field. Read and learn. The more you know, the more your cottage company will profit.

Step 2. Know your customers. Businesses succeed when they find a need and fill it. That means you must know your customers and what they want. Maybe you've been a customer for this service yourself. What did you expect from it? How would you improve it? If you haven't used the service, do you know someone who has? If so, what did they expect? Find out who will buy your service, why, how, when, for how much, and other facts. The more you know about your customer, the more you will sell.

Step 3. Know the law. Business laws promote fair trade and public health. Contact your city and state/provincial government to learn what laws your cottage company is required to follow. Some cities don't allow home businesses, especially if customers come to your home. Most cities require business licenses and other filings. You'll probably need a health license if you prepare or sell food. You'll also have to pay income taxes on the profits of your business. In the U.S., start your search by checking the phone book's white pages under "Small Business Development Center." It can help you learn the laws for your location and cottage company.

Step 4. Know your assets. You may have more assets to start your cottage company than you realize. Besides your skills, talents, knowledge, experience and some savings, you may have another valuable asset: time. Make a list of these assets, including time available to you. When I started my part-time writing business many years ago, I wrote each morning before going to work at my regular job. I also wrote during my lunch hour.

Step 5. Add real value. Whatever cottage you select, you must give real value to your service. A secretarial service offers free pick up and delivery. A pet sitter spends at least one hour each day training the animal in obedience. A bookkeeper prepares tax forms at no extra charge for all clients who have signed an annual contract. Do more than your customers expect—and more than your competitors do— and your cottage company will succeed.

Step 6. Keep good customers. Frankly, some of your customers will be easier to help than others. A few will be very difficult to satisfy. One or two will forget to pay you. Once you've identified which customers are the most profitable and most enjoyable to serve, work hard to keep them. Build a friendly relationship with them. Find out if there are related services you can offer them. Find out if their friends and relatives need your services. Keeping and profiting from good customers will help you afford dropping those who aren't so good for your business.

Step 7. Manage money wisely. As money starts coming in from your cottage company, it's easy to forget that it's not all yours. You'll have to share some of it with the telephone company, your supplier, the tax collector and others. You'll only be able to keep a fraction of every dollar. To keep a larger fraction, you must manage your money wisely by keeping expenses to a minimum while increasing opportunities for income. How? The biggest thief of cottage dollars is impulse buying. You see a product or service advertised that you think you must have to operate. It may be a computer or software or a special tool. And you may be correct; the expense may bring you many more cottage dollars. Or it may not. To minimize impulse purchases, keep a list of potential purchases with the date on which you will decide. The date should be at least 30 days from when you add it to your list. In the meantime, make a note on the list every time you would have used it if you had it. By the end of the period you'll know whether the purchase will be profitable or not.

Step 8. Do it better. Doing something well isn't good enough anymore. You must do it *better*. You must do it better than competitors do it. And you must do it better than you did it last month. How can you improve your service? By continually improving your knowledge of your business, its customers and the law, by increasing and using your assets, by adding value to your service, by making and keeping good customers and by managing your money better every day.

Where to find the money you need

A recent survey of small businesses reported that 23 percent had lines of credit, 7 percent had financial leases, 14 percent had mortgage loans, 12 percent had equipment loans and 25 percent had vehicle loans. For larger firms, the percentages about double in each category.

The ability to get a loan when you need it is as necessary to the operation of your business as is the right equipment. Before a bank or any other lending agency will lend you money, the loan officer must feel satisfied with the answers to these five questions:

1. What sort of person are you, the prospective borrower? In most cases, the character of the borrower comes first. Next is your ability to manage your business.

2. What are you going to do with the money? The answer to this question will determine the type of loan and the duration.

3. When and how do you plan to pay it back? Your lender's judgment of your business ability and the type of loan will be a deciding factor in the answer to this question.

4. Is the cushion in the loan large enough? In other words, does the amount requested make suitable allowance for unexpected developments? The lender decides this question on the basis of your financial statement, which sets forth the condition of your business, and on the collateral pledged.

5. What's the outlook for business in general and for your business in particular?

When you set out to borrow money for your firm, it is important to know the kind of money you need from a bank or other lending institution. Let's discuss loans and other types of credit. There are numerous types of loans available, all with their own unique name depending on the lender.

Signature loan. A signature loan holds nothing in collateral except your promise to pay the lender back on terms with which you both agree. If your monetary needs are small, you need the loan only for a short time, your credit rating is excellent and you're willing to pay a premium interest rate because you're not using physical collateral, a signature or character loan is an easy way to borrow money in a hurry.

Credit cards. Many a small business has found at least some of its funding in the owner's personal credit card. Computers, printers, books, office supplies, office overhead and other costs can be covered with your personal credit card. However, interest rates on credit cards are extremely high—sometimes double what you might pay on a collateral loan. But credit cards can offer you quick cash when you need it. If this is an option for you, talk to your credit card representative about raising your credit limit. It will be much easier to do so while you're employed by someone else.

Line of credit. A line of credit is similar to a loan, except that you don't borrow it all at once. You get a credit limit, say $20,000, that you can tap anytime you need money for business purposes. The most common is the revolving line of credit that you can draw from when business is off and pay back when business is good, providing that you don't exceed your limit. A line of credit is an excellent way for a home business to work through the ups and downs of seasonal business. With some restrictions, a line of credit can be established using a portion of your home equity as collateral. Using a secured equity earns you a lower interest rate.

Cosigner loan. A cosigner loan should be one of the most popular loans for small businesses, but many business people never consider it. Put simply, you find a cosigner or a comaker with good credit or assets who will guarantee the loan with you. If you have a potential investor who believes in your business but doesn't want to put up the cash you need, ask him or her to cosign a loan with you. Your chances of receiving the loan are much better. Some cosigners will require that you pay them a fee of 1 to 4 percent of the balance or a flat fee. Others will do it out of friendship or the hope of future business from you. In any case, consider this an excellent source of capital for your new home business.

Equipment leases. If you're purchasing equipment, computers or other assets for your business, the supplier may loan or lease the equipment to you. This often requires about 25 percent down, so be ready to come up with some cash of your own.

Collateral loan. A collateral loan is one in which some type of asset is put up as collateral; if you don't make payments you will lose the asset. The lender wants to make sure that the value of the asset exceeds that of the loan, and will usually lend 50 to 75 percent of asset value. A new home business owner often does not have sufficient collateral—real estate or equipment—to secure a collateral loan unless an owner uses personal assets, such as a home.

Pass book loan. Sometimes you can get a loan by assigning a savings account to the bank. In such cases, the bank gets an assignment from you and keeps your pass book. If you assign an account in another bank as collateral, the lending bank asks the other bank to mark its records to show that the account is held as collateral.

Life insurance loan. Another kind of collateral is life insurance. Banks will lend up to the cash value of a life insurance policy. You have to assign the policy to the bank. If the policy is on an executive of a small corporation, corporate resolutions must be made authorizing the assignment. Most insurance companies allow you to sign the policy back to the original beneficiary when the assignment to the bank ends. Some people like to use life insurance as collateral rather than borrow directly from insurance companies. One reason is that a bank loan is often more convenient to obtain and may often be obtained at a lower interest rate.

Making sure your business is legal

Depending on the type of home business you start, its size and location, you will need one or more licenses or permits from one or more governments. Some businesses require more licenses than others. I'll talk about general licensing requirements here and in the cottage profiles in Part 2. You should check with local government on other requirements.

Licenses give you the right to operate a business as long as you follow the rules. Licenses are a necessary nuisance. Without them, anyone could set up a business on a street corner and rob customers of thousands of dollars without recourse. Though not perfect, business licensing systems at least reduce the chances of this happening and attempt to instill trust in buyers. Typically, it's state, county and municipal governments that issue business licenses. Check your regional telephone book for government business licensing offices.

In addition to a business license, you may also need to file the name of your business. A fictitious or assumed business name is a name other than the real and true name of each person operating a business. A real and true name becomes an assumed business name with the addition of any words that imply the existence of additional owners. For example, Mary Smith is a real and true name, while Mary Smith Company is an assumed business name.

In many states, an assumed business name is registered with the state's corporate division. Some states will also register your assumed business name with counties in which you do business. Other states require that you do so. In some locations, you must publish a public notice in an area newspaper, saying that you (and any other business principals) are operating under a specific business name.

The typical assumed business name registration requires the business name you wish to assume, the principal place of business, the name of an authorized representative, your SIC (standard industrial classification) code, a list of all owners with their signatures and a list of all counties in which your firm will transact business. Of course, there will also be a registration fee. To help, I'll include the SIC code for many of the cottage profiles.

Some cottage companies also require professional licenses or permits, such as for those who buy, sell, build or repair houses, those who work with food and those who transport products for others. Your state business office can help you decide whether you need such a license or permit and how to apply. Some professions will also require special insurance or bonding. I'll mention some of them in the profiles.

Your city or town may also have zoning regulations that limit the type of business that operates in a residential area. Most zoning laws simply limit potential traffic in a residential neighborhood. However, others discourage any type of business based in a home. Contact local zoning offices to find out what is allowed and what isn't.

You will have to pay your governments for the privilege of running a cottage company. How much tax, to whom and when, depend on what you sell, to whom you sell, how much you profit, whether you have inventory or employees and other factors. You may also be required to collect and pass along sales tax on your product or service.

One more item: Remember that, under normal circumstances, your home business won't be covered under your homeowner's insurance policy. Inventory you keep in the garage, extra computer equipment and the safety of customers typically require additional insurance. Once you've decided on your cottage company, talk to your insurance agent about extended coverage.

Don't turn your home into a crazy house

Bringing a business into your home can sometimes work havoc on both. This is especially true if you share your home with a spouse, children, relatives and/or pets. How can you reduce the big problems to manageable ones? Here are some practical and proven tips for those who want to start and operate a cottage company:

Tip #1: Find a place to work. The hardest part of working at home is facing the distractions of housework, coffee with neighbors and Oprah. My first home office was set up in a walk-in closet. Another was in a travel trailer in our driveway. Kitchen tables or other multi-purpose locations don't work for very long. Find a quiet space to establish your cottage company. Make sure others in your home know when you cannot be disturbed for nonbusiness activities.

Tip #2: Find a time to work. We all have many demands on our time. But if we don't set aside time for something important to us, it will never get done. I operated one of my earliest cottage companies working two hours every evening and four hours over the weekend. Now I'm in my home office from 8 a.m. to 5 p.m., Monday through Friday. If I work a few hours over the weekend, I take some time off the following week. Use the time in your office efficiently.

Tip #3: Find a focus. Imagine an announcement that McDonalds was now selling groceries as well. It won't happen, because McDonalds knows—as other successful businesses know—that you must find a focus and stay with it to be successful. If your cottage company writes resumes *and* waxes cars, you're not focused enough to do either one well. Focus.

Tip #4: Have fun. Why work in the home if you can't have some fun from time to time? Enjoy what you're doing, why you're doing it and for whom. As much as possible, make each work day a pleasant experience.

That reminds me: I have to stop writing for now so I can go watch our son's wresting match. See you in Chapter 2!

Chapter 2

How to plan
your success

Success is a destination, but it is also a journey. Like all successful journeys, you must plan where you are going, how you will get there, what it will cost and what you will do while you're there. That's what this second chapter is about: planning for the success of your cottage company.

How to plan

If you were planning a trip from, say, Chicago, you would first identify your destination—maybe San Francisco. Then you would figure out the best way to get there: airplane, bus, car, bicycle, walking, etc. If by plane or bus, you'd find out which common carriers make the trip between the two cities. If by a private motor vehicle, you'd look at a map for the highway that will get you there the quickest. You would then calculate the distance between the two points (about 2,200 miles), the time required for the trip and major stops along the way. You'd figure the costs, the time required and some sights to see.

Planning the success of your cottage company requires the same kind of planning. To make a good plan—one that has the greatest chances of success—you will learn what the business does, what's needed to start, who your customers are, how to price your product or service and how much you will make. Those are the topics of this chapter. First, let's talk about how you can discover the best opportunity to meet your needs and the needs of your potential customers.

How to discover the best opportunity

About 57 percent of all Americans—and almost two-thirds of those under 30—would rather own their own business than work for someone else. Yet Dun & Bradstreet reports that 28 percent of all new businesses fail within the first three years, and 63 percent fail within six years. It can also be the American nightmare! Here are 10 vital steps to making your own business a success.

Step 1. List five things you do best. Include trades, skills, hobbies, interests and activities. Review your life for unfulfilled dreams, as well as opportunities for growth. You may enjoy working with flowers or organizing travel excursions.

Step 2. List how other people would benefit from what you do best. To be profitable, a business must offer valuable products or services to others. For example, if you are best at working with flowers, you can help others grow them, select them, arrange them, sell them, prepare them or maintain them. In each case, others will benefit from what you do. The more they benefit, the more you will profit.

Step 3. Find out how to give people what they want. Where can you get the tools and materials you will need? If you want to help others with travel, for example, you'll need to learn what travel-related businesses are available, how to find customers, how to find travel resources and how to make a profit at it. You will want to clearly understand the business's "process," its requirements and its output.

Step 4. Discover the value of your services to others. What are people willing or able to pay for your products or services? If you're not already so, become a customer of the type of business you want to start. That is, if you want to become a computer consultant, come up with a problem you would typically solve and begin interviewing computer consultants about what they do and how much they charge to solve the problem. Also interview people who might become your customers. Find out what they want and how much they pay for it.

Step 5. Find out who else offers similar services. Every business has competition. Check the local telephone book and national trade magazines to find your potential competitors. If possible, become their customer, or at least contact them for more information on what they do and how they do it. You should know more about your competitors than your customers do.

Step 6. Learn from the successes of others. You'll quickly identify your most successful competitors. By becoming one of their customers you can learn more about how they started, what they do well and how well they are. Ask your regional reference librarian how to find newspaper and magazine articles about your competitors.

Step 7. Learn from the failures of others. As you learn more about your business opportunity, you'll hear about businesses that didn't succeed. In each case, track them down and learn from their mistakes. If you can't find the owners, find and talk with its customers to learn why the business failed.

Step 8. Plan your own success. You know what you want to do, what others are willing to pay for, how to give it to them and how to succeed. Pull it all together in your business plan. Write it all down in a notebook, including financial requirements, resources, estimated income and expenses and other important facts. Keep adding to and revising your plan until it's the best it can be. Then do it!

Step 9. Make low-cost mistakes. Business mistakes are inevitable. In fact, if you're not making a few mistakes in business, you're not trying hard enough! However, make *inexpensive* mistakes and learn valuable lessons from each one. One part-time floral service operated in a garage until business was sufficiently built to rent a retail store. By then, the owner had made hundreds of small mistakes—and profited from nearly every one of them.

Step 10. Enjoy what you do and how you do it. Life is too short to spend it doing something you don't enjoy or doing it for the wrong reasons. Enjoying your business simply requires reducing stressful worry. There's always something to worry about in business, but it doesn't have to stop you from enjoying your enterprise and your life.

What will I be doing?

Okay. You've looked at the discovery process. It's now time to answer the questions that all cottage companies must answer:

- What will I be doing?
- What will I need to start?
- Who will my customers be?
- How much should I charge?
- How much will I make?

First, let's tackle the question of what you'll be doing. Whatever it is, it will be a *process*. All businesses, large and small, have a process. A process is a series of operations required in making a product or furnishing a service. The process of making a hamburger, for example, requires knowledge (how to prepare), materials (meat, bun, pickle, special sauce) and labor (cooking, assembling, packaging), and results in a specific output (a hamburger) in a form that the customer wants.

Think about the processes that you've already participated in. Maybe you've made or sold hamburgers at a fast food restaurant. Or maybe you've worked in a paper mill, helping process wood chips into paper. You may have experience as a receptionist in a professional office, processing requests into appointments and appointments into billing charges. In each case, you process one thing into another thing that adds value. The more value you add, the more you're paid.

Filling out an Opportunity Worksheet (see page 176) will help you study the processes that you've already been in and what you've learned from them. You'll consider the purpose of each process, its inputs, what you did to add value, the outputs and who benefited from them enough to exchange money for them.

What will I need to start?

There are certain things you'll need to start any cottage company:

◆ Knowledge of the product or service you will provide.

◆ Skills to add value to the product or service.

◆ Resources and equipment to help you add value.

◆ People or other businesses who will buy what you produce.

Your Resource Worksheet (see page 177) will help you clarify what you already have in the way of knowledge, skills, resources and potential customers. You can also use it to compare with the requirements of the part-time cottage companies included in this book.

How much money will you need to start your cottage company? Of course, you must know this before you select your business. If you can afford only a few hundred dollars, you don't want to start a business that requires $20,000 to set up.

To estimate start-up costs, you will need to make your best guess of how much it will cost to set up your office. This includes the cost of preparing and equipping your office, getting required licenses and professional memberships, getting the phone hooked up and paying for your initial advertising.

Estimating operating costs can be difficult, because it requires that you estimate your living expenses as well. Most people who have been employees spend as much as they make. They're not sure exactly what they *need* to live on. However, by starting with your current net (after tax) salary, you can roughly calculate whether you require more or less to live on. If you operate your business as a proprietor, your income tax and self-employment (social security) tax will be paid by the business.

Other operating costs are those expenses that you will pay each month to keep the doors open (fixed or overhead expenses), as well as those that increase as sales increase (variable expenses).

Who will my customers be?

Every business, large or small, must have customers—someone to buy what they produce. The lack of customers is probably the greatest reason why businesses fail. You can produce the best products or services, but if there are no customers for them or the customers don't know about your efforts, you will soon be out of business.

The best way to understand your customers is to interview them. Find out what they are thinking. Understand what they want from a home business and from you. Ask them what is most important to them. Learn what makes them select one home business over another. Talk with friends who have recently bought or used what you will be selling. In general, you'll learn that your customers want a product or service that gives them a value greater than the cost.

Who your customers will be depends on what you're making and selling. Your customers could be individuals, groups, professionals, retail buyers, wholesalers, manufacturers, schools, governments or others. Your Customer Worksheet (see page 178) will help you determine what type of customers you prefer and have experience working with. You can then compare these facts to the specific cottage profiles in this book to learn what customers you would work best with.

How much should I charge?

To set the price of your product or service, you need information about the cost of materials, the time required to make the piece, the cost of overhead and the amount of profit you should reasonably expect. Let's look at each of these components in brief.

Material cost is the cost of the materials used directly in the final product. Supplies are usually part of overhead and not material cost. However, the cost of picking up materials or having them shipped to you is a part of the cost of the materials, rather than overhead.

Labor cost is the cost of work directly applied to making the product or service. Labor not directly applied to making the product is an overhead cost. Labor cost includes both the hourly wage and the cost of any fringe benefits.

Overhead is the indirect cost of making your product, expenses that aren't consumed by making the product or producing the service. For example, the cost of an office is an overhead expense. If you have purchased this book to make a profit with your product—which I assume you have—the cost of the book is an indirect cost and can be deducted from your taxes as a legitimate business expense. It is a part of your overhead.

Finally, *profit* is the amount of money you have left over once you've paid all the bills. Many small business owners who have invested hundreds or even thousands of dollars into their equipment and their skills never consider that they should receive a return on that investment. They would never think of renting money to a bank interest-free, but they will to their business. A fair profit is vital to the success of your enterprise. Without it, your home business may not be here a year from now to serve new customers.

Establishing your hourly service rate is a simple process of adding overhead and expected profit to the cost of labor. That is, if you want to pay yourself $15 per hour and a benefits package worth $5 per hour, add to this your overhead, say $5 an hour, and your expected profit, such as 20 percent of the labor/benefits/overhead cost or $5. You come up with a total of $30 per hour. You then apply this hourly rate to the work you do.

One popular method of pricing products and services is called *markup*. Markup is a percentage of the materials cost that is added to cover labor and operating expenses. As an example, a cake decorator may add 300 percent of the cost of materials as the cost of labor, another 100 percent for the cost of equipment (oven, pans, supplies, etc.) and another 100 percent for profit. That is a total markup of 500 percent or five times the materials cost. If the materials for a wedding cake cost $15, the markup is $75 ($15 x 5) and the total price is $90 ($15 + $75). Does that mean the profit on this job is 100 percent? Not at all. It's actually $15 (100 percent x the materials cost of $15) or about 16.66 percent of the total price of $90. The profit is then just over 16 percent.

Another way of looking at markup pricing is to establish a "rule of thumb." In the previous example, the rule of thumb is to price the job at five times the materials cost (100 percent of materials cost + 500 percent for markup = 600 percent or 6X).

Your Price Analysis Worksheet (see page 179) will help you determine your cottage company's hourly rate and per-job rate.

How much will I make?

That depends on your profit, which is simply the amount of money you have left over once you've paid all of your expenses. If you have more expenses than income, you have a loss. Pretty simple. Of course, there's much more to profit and loss than numbers on paper. Your business can actually show a profit on paper, yet not have any cash. In fact, many profitable companies go out of business each year because of negative cash flow.

How can you keep the cash flowing in your home business? By keeping good records, watching expenses and tracking the flow of cash in and out of your business. Your Income and Expense Worksheet (see page 180) will help you determine how much of the money you make you can keep.

Part 2

How to start the right weekend business

We've arrived. In Part 1 of this book you considered starting a part-time home business and analyzed your experiences and skills. You can now compare your self-analysis to 101 proven, successful businesses to find one that's right for you.

The opportunities described in this section aren't theoretical. They are actual home businesses. My descriptions of them are based on interviews with home business owners and my own experiences throughout three decades of owning and managing small businesses.

Among these home ventures, I sincerely hope you find an opportunity to meet your financial and personal needs—whether over the weekend or all week long.

Aerobics instructor

What will I be doing?

An aerobics instructor gets paid to help others perspire. Actually, an aerobics instructor helps others exercise in their home, a commercial gym, a dance studio or the instructor's own studio. It's an excellent part-time job because many customers want the services of an instructor after work or on weekends. Based on need, you may decide to expand this venture into full-time or to add personal weight management or related services.

What will I need to start?

You don't need your own studio to begin a part-time aerobics class. You can start in your home, a remodeled garage or a rented studio. Aerobics is physical exercise that doesn't require special equipment, so your initial investment will be minimal. You should have both knowledge and experience of aerobics and related exercise methods. In fact, you can use your experience and credentials to help you promote your new part-time business by offering exercise tips in local newspapers.

Who will my customers be?

Most people want to slim down or increase energy and fitness. Depending on local need and competition, you can offer aerobic training to beginners, intermediates or advanced customers. You can also focus on a type of exercise, such as Jazzercize or low-impact aerobics, or you can focus on the needs of a group of customers, such as seniors or toddlers. To find customers who need your help, learn which classes are now being offered in your area and look for an aerobics need that you can fulfill.

How much should I charge?

Pricing your aerobics instruction is actually quite easy. You don't need much equipment, so you can base most of your fee on an a fair hourly rate. Newer instructors establish a rate of $20 to $25 an hour, while more experienced and well-known instructors charge $35 to $40 an hour. Studio rental, even if it's in your home, is added to this. Use this fee to calculate your price per session. For example, if you have 10 students for an hour three times a week, add up the total number of hours per week (three), multiply it by your fee ($30/hour), then divide it by the number of students, for a per-student rate ($9). Make sure you include setup time.

How much will I make?

Most of the time, an aerobics instructor is paid at the hourly rate. Only about 10 to 20 percent of the instructor's time is needed for marketing, and thus is not billable. So if you have 10 hours a week that you can devote to aerobics instruction, you should be able to sell eight or nine hours of it once you get the business started. Overhead costs are small, typically about 10 to 25 percent, depending on whether you're renting a studio and how you're advertising your services.

How can I get started?

To start your part-time aerobics instruction business, learn about your competitors, find a group of customers you want to serve, find a place to exercise together, calculate your pricing and jump in.

Alterations service

What will I be doing?

In this era of "disposable" clothing, there are still many people who know the value of quality. They buy better clothing, then have it altered or tailored to meet their needs. Others extend the life of quality garments with alterations. A few even have clothing custom-made. A part-time alterations service can meet these needs.

What will I need to start?

An alterations service requires few tools beyond a quality sewing machine. However, advanced sewing skills and a knowledge of clothing design can help ensure efficiency and success. Most alterations services offer zipper repair and replacement, hemming and waist alteration. Others specialize in alterations that require advanced equipment or skills. To enhance your skills, take advanced clothing classes or apprentice at a tailor shop where you can learn techniques that are nearly lost.

Who will my customers be?

There are more than 9,600 full-time alterations services in the U.S. and many thousands more that are operated part-time. These part-time businesses typically offer basic alterations services through advertisements in local newspapers and shoppers guides. Others work as subcontractors to finer clothing stores, tailors and related businesses. Depending on available time, some alterations services do both, especially if one type of alteration work is more seasonal than another.

How much should I charge?

Alterations services typically establish an hourly rate of $20 to $45, depending on specialty, skills and competition. However, they usually charge customers by the piece. Zipper replacement is priced by the inch of length. Hems are priced by the garment. Specialty work is priced by the hour, but quoted to the customer by the job.

How much will I make?

It's doubtful that anyone has become rich with an alterations service. However, for people who enjoy sewing, helping others and working at home, an alterations service can offer a good part-time income. In most cases, nearly all of your time is chargeable, once the business is established. Overhead expense (equipment, materials, telephone, taxes, etc.) is usually 15 to 30 percent. Word-of-mouth advertising for quality work minimizes advertising costs and increases profitable repeat business.

How can I get started?

The first step to starting an alterations service is to make sure you are fast and efficient. If you have lots of interest in this venture, but little experience, volunteer to do free alterations for a consignment or resale clothing store. Then, when you feel ready, use the store as a reference to get other jobs with new clothing stores. Also read competitors' advertisements and learn who is successful and why.

The SIC code for alterations services is 5699-32.

Antique appraiser

What will I be doing?

Antiques are valuable. Antiques include furniture, automobiles, collectibles and other items from earlier times. The value of antiques lies in the uniqueness, quality and desirability of each item. Though establishing a current value for antiques is somewhat arbitrary, there are value guides and guidelines that can be used to make your job easier. What you're selling as an antique appraiser is your knowledge.

What will I need to start?

To sell your knowledge you must have it. That is, if you're appraising antique cars, you must know as much or more about these cars and their current value as nearly anyone. You must know not only the finer points of the original product, but also the prices of similar products around the country. You must read, interview, study, analyze, record and remember.

Who will my customers be?

Who cares what the current value of an antique is? Many people: sellers, buyers, investors, auction companies, insurance companies and the general public. These are your customers. For example, you may decide to become an expert appraiser in Shaker furniture, developing such a knowledge that you help investors earn money buying and selling undervalued pieces. Or you can help owners or insurance agents establish fair market value for antiques in case of loss.

How much should I charge?

As with most services, antique appraisers establish a fair hourly rate for their time and knowledge, but quote prices to customers in other ways. The most typical pricing is as a flat fee or a percentage of value. For example, you may value all items in an estate for the executor or an auction company. Your price could be $500 or, say, 3 percent of the estate's value. The exact fee or percent will vary depending on what services you perform, your credentials and your competition. The hourly rate for a part-time appraiser ranges from $25 to $60.

How much will I make?

As an established part-time antique appraiser, most of your time will be paid for by a client. You won't have to spend much time marketing your services. But you will spend 15 to 30 percent of your time renewing your knowledge, reading up on your field, attending auctions and increasing the value of your expertise. The overhead cost of developing this knowledge and paying home office and some travel expenses will be about 10 to 20 percent. Add in about the same to pay taxes, depending on state and local taxation of your business.

How can I get started?

To sell your expertise you must first develop your knowledge. Learn as much as you can about your field of antiques. If possible, find a part-time job working for an appraiser or volunteer your services to a charitable group so you can gain experience. Find, purchase and study valuation guides for your field. Then, once you're ready, contact potential customers through telephone calls, advertising and publicity to let them know of your services and fees.

Antique restoration service

What will I be doing?

If you have the skills to restore antiques to their former beauty, you can make a good part- or full-time income with an antique restoration service. There are more than 5,800 full-time antique restoration services in the U.S., and probably double that number of part-timers making extra money with an enjoyable business. They find, repair, restore and refinish furniture, automobiles, collectibles and other products of the past.

What will I need to start?

Restoring antiques requires a variety of related and highly developed skills. If you decide to restore antique furniture, you'll need to have a working knowledge of woods, old and new finishes, finishing techniques and other skills. You will also need woodworking and wood finishing tools. If you're restoring cars, you'll need an even wider variety of skills, tools, techniques and knowledge. Many people start this business as a hobby until they have gained enough knowledge, skills, resources and equipment to attract paying customers.

Who will my customers be?

Your antique restoration knowledge and skills will be sold to individuals, antique dealers, resellers, estates, investors, galleries, museums and others. Your specific customers will depend on what types of antiques you restore, your experience and local opportunities.

How much should I charge?

Antique restoration services typically earn $35 to $75 or more an hour. The wide variation of rates is based on a variation in skills and the tools required. Some restoration services can manage with a hundred dollars in hand tools, while others will need an investment of many thousands of dollars to do a quality job. Most restoration services are priced on the value added. That is, a rough antique worth $100 that is restored into one worth $1000 should earn the restorer a fee based on the increased value, rather than just the time and tools needed.

How much will I make?

Once established, an antique restoration service requires only about 10 to 20 percent of the owner's time to sell and keep the books. However, overhead expenses can be higher than other home businesses, because of the investment in tools and equipment. Total overhead, including taxes, may be as high as 50 cents of every dollar.

How can I get started?

To start a part-time antique restoration service, many people find, restore and resell pieces on their own. Skills are then developed, resources are found and a profit is made. Others start this venture by working for someone else.

The SIC code for antique restoration services is 7641-12.

Apartment preparation service

What will I be doing?

Apartments are everywhere. They fill a need for millions of people who frequently move or can't afford to buy their own home. An apartment preparation service cleans and repairs apartments between tenants. An apartment preparation service is on-call and must respond quickly to customers, especially because most customers will own or rent many apartments over the years and can help you build your business.

What will I need to start?

Your part-time apartment prep business can specialize in cleaning, repair or both services. If the business is run by a couple, each partner may specialize in one type of service. Some jobs may require calling in an electrical, painting, drywall or plumbing contractor.

Tools and supplies needed depend on what you're doing. However, minimum tools are those you may already have in your home: vacuum, broom, mop, pail, brushes, cleaning supplies, etc.

Who will my customers be?

Customers for your apartment preparation service include apartment managers, owners, property managers, real estate agents and renters. Most of your work will come from apartment owners and managers, though you may sometimes be called on by a renter who wants an apartment cleaned to get a large deposit back. You can contact potential customers by developing a single-page brochure or flier on your services, including prices, and taking it to all apartment and real estate offices in your area. Return to each location about every three months, as needs and employees change.

How much should I charge?

The hourly rate for apartment preparation service varies, depending on what tasks are being done. Most services establish a rate of $25 to $35 an hour for cleaning and $30 to $50 an hour for repairs. Sometimes the repairs can be subcontracted to another home business with a finders fee kept by the prep service. Eestimate the work required to clean and/or repair a typical apartment, then establish a rate based on the number of rooms or the square feet in the apartment. Make sure your rate is comparable with your competitor's. Some prep services offer a discount to apartment owners who agree to a specific amount of services during a period of time.

How much will I make?

Marketing your apartment preparation service will take at least 25 percent of your time as you start your business, then be reduced as you develop repeat and referral business. Calculate the cost of supplies for cleaning a typical apartment and make sure you include it in your pricing. About 30 to 50 percent of every dollar you charge will go to supplies, equipment, taxes and other overhead expenses.

How can I get started?

The skills required to operate an apartment preparation service are minimal and many can be learned on the job. One way of starting is to talk with an apartment manager to learn what is expected and how much is typically paid, then offer to do the same job for 25 to 50 percent less if the manager will show you what needs to be done. A few apartments like this and you'll soon be as much of an expert in apartment prep as anyone.

Aquarium maintenance service

What will I be doing?

There's something tranquil about watching fish in an aquarium. That's why you may have seen an aquarium in many professional offices and some restaurants, where a relaxing mood is important. In most cases, though, the doctor or the maitre d' is not the person who cleans and maintains the tank. If the tank is large or the fish are expensive, an aquarium maintenance service probably does the work. This is especially true of delicate and costly saltwater aquariums.

If you enjoy and have a knowledge of aquarium care, this may be an excellent part-time business for you.

What will I need to start?

Of course, to care for fish and aquariums, you must know something about them. More than from a book, you must have some experience with aquarium setup and equipment, fish selection and health and their environmental requirements. You will also need some resources (books, names of experts) and equipment (siphons, isolation tanks). In addition, you will need reliable sources for food, medicines, aquariums and new or replacement fish.

Who will my customers be?

Your customers will include offices, restaurants and retail stores. It will also include individuals who have or want large aquariums in their homes, but don't want the maintenance problems. How can you find customers for your aquarium maintenance service? Many places. First, select aquarium supply stores and pet stores that your potential customers might use. Then market your services to the store owner, offering a finders fee for new customers or offering to buy your supplies at the store. Also, develop and mail a brochure about your services to potential customers. Use the local telephone book or buy a mailing list from a list broker to get the addresses of professional offices, restaurants and retail stores.

How much should I charge?

Your service is valuable, but many may perceive it to be a minimum-wage job. It certainly isn't. Dressing the part in an inexpensive uniform embroidered with your business name on the back will help to promote your business and your value.

The typical hourly rate for an aquarium maintenance service is $20 to $35 depending on what services are provided. In addition, a mileage charge may be added to cover travel expenses between customers. But customers don't want your hourly rate, they want your price. So you calculate what time a standard or extended service call will take, multiply it by your hourly rate, add mileage if necessary, and that's your price.

For example, a weekly feeding of a set of large tanks may take 20 minutes of your time. At $30 an hour, 20 minutes is worth $10. Adding a mileage charge of 5 miles times 30 cents a mile is $1.50. Multiply the total by 52 weeks a year and divide by 12 months to get a monthly price of $49.83. Call it $50 a month. You may want to charge slightly more for a maintenance contract shorter than one year.

How much will I make?

You have few out-of-pocket expenses with your aquarium maintenance service. The customer buys the food and supplies. You may need some transportation, but you can adjust your charge accordingly.

Once your business is developed, you won't have to advertise much. So most of your time will be billable to a customer. If your business takes six hours each week at $25 an hour, your gross income is $150 a week or $7,800 a year. Overhead expenses (uniform, some equipment and supplies) will take about 10 percent of that and taxes will take another 15 to 20 percent. The rest is yours.

How can I get started?

The first step to starting your aquarium maintenance service is to begin thinking like a customer. Check the telephone book and newspaper for such services. Find out who your competitors are, what they do, how much they charge and where they serve. Then design your own business to do it better. If you don't already have them, begin gathering books on aquarium maintenance and on fish.

Art broker/agent

What will I be doing?

If you enjoy art and want to be a part of the process, consider becoming an art broker or agent. You don't have to live in Manhattan or even be near a major gallery to do so. You can be an art broker from your home. And you can do it in your spare time.

An art broker or agent buys and sell works of art or crafts for others on commission or consignment. You can represent the buyers or the sellers or both. You can specialize in investment art, classical art, craft products or other elements of the art world.

What will I need to start?

An art broker or agent doesn't really sell art. He or she sells knowledge: knowledge of art, of buyers and sellers, of pricing, of negotiation and of people. If you don't have this knowledge, get it. Learn as much as you can not only about art, but also about the commerce (buying and selling) of art. If you can, get some experience working for an art broker, even if it's in a clerical position.

Who will my customers be?

Who will buy art and crafts from you? Your customers will be art investors and managers of professional offices and fine restaurants, as well as other artists. Yes, some artists, as they become more well-known and affluent, may want to buy the art that appeals to them. How can you reach these customers? By becoming more involved in local and regional art shows, artist's groups and small galleries, you'll meet many people who want to buy or sell art. Listen, learn, take notes, advise, ask, and soon you will be developing a group of customers.

How much should I charge?

An established art broker makes good money—typically $40 to $100 an hour. Those starting out may not make quite as much, but if you enjoy the work, it's still good money. Of course, most art brokers don't quote their prices as an hourly rate. They do the math in their head and offer the price with a commission or finders fee of 5 to 20 percent. About 10 percent is typical. Another 10 percent may be tacked on to allow for negotiations. So, a painting the artist will sell for $400 is priced at $500 with a bottom price of $450. If the art broker uses a gallery (most part-timers don't), the fee is typically 25 to 50 percent of the total price ($600 to $800 for the artist's $400 painting).

How much will I make?

About a third of your time as an art broker or agent will be spent on learning, and thus not directly billable to any client. That's one reason for the higher hourly rate: to cover unbillable time. Another 10 to 20 percent will be required to cover your overhead costs. So about half of each dollar you bring in will go into your pocket to keep. Maybe less. Even so, a part-time art broker working eight hours a week can bring in $16,000 to $30,000 a year and keep half of it. This is an especially lucrative business for those with contacts in the world of art.

How can I get started?

Starting your art brokerage is simple enough: Print some business cards and begin handing them out. Making a profit at what you do will mean learning, gathering information, following up, making new friends and being genuinely helpful. Also take advantage of opportunities to promote yourself and your business through newspaper feature stories about the local art world. You may even decide to write a regular column for a regional art magazine to show everyone that you're an expert.

Auto detail service

What will I be doing?

This is a business you'll either love or hate. If you enjoy cars and enjoy making them look their best, you'll love this job. Otherwise, they couldn't pay you enough to do it. It's hard work.

An auto detail service professionally cleans, washes, waxes and maintains the interior and exterior surfaces of cars, trucks, RVs and other vehicles. There are more than 11,000 full-time auto detail services in the U.S., with thousands more operated from homes and garages.

What will I need to start?

To start an auto detailing service, all you really need is some time. You can begin by offering to wash and clean cars at a local car lot for an hourly rate or for a fee per car. This is good on-the-job self-training. If you already have experience waxing and cleaning cars, you can apply this knowledge to your new business. If you know something about automotive paints and touch-up, all the better.

Equipment is minimal. You can buy a power buffer later. For now, purchase quality wash, wax and interior cleaning products. Use a washing bucket to hold everything. You'll soon learn which products work best for you at the lowest cost. Once learned, you can buy your products at wholesale or bulk prices.

Who will my customers be?

Who wants their vehicles cleaned and renewed? Your customers will include new car owners, classic car owners, new and used car dealers, trailer and motor home owners and dealers, boat owners and dealers and others. You can specialize in one or more areas or you may prefer to work with a variety of vehicles.

How can you find customers? Place a small ad in the automotive section of a local newspaper. Print fliers about your services, distribute them in parking lots and to car dealers, and post them on bulletin boards.

How much should I charge?

The hourly rate for an automotive detailer depends somewhat on your level of skills, as well as on the value of the vehicle you're detailing. Cleaning clunker cars on a budget car lot won't earn you much, maybe $20 to $25 an hour if you work efficiently. However, detailing and touching up valuable new or classic cars can get you $35 to $50 an hour. As with other home-based businesses, use your hourly rate to calculate the price of a typical job. For example, a detailing that requires 45 minutes at $30 an hour should be priced at about $22.50.

How much will I make?

Once established, you'll spend only about 10 to 20 percent of your time marketing your business. The rest of the time will be spent detailing cars. Because you work out of your home, garage or your own vehicle, your expenses are minimal. Detailing materials may cost $3 to $5 an hour. Overhead, including taxes, may take about 20 to 30 percent of every dollar you get. The other dollars are yours.

How can I get started?

First, learn your trade. Work as a detailer for a car lot, or practice on your own and friends' cars. Read up on the subject. Have your car detailed by a service and watch how they do it. Also watch what products they use and how long it takes to use them.

Here's an idea for promoting your detailing service: One new detailer used a family car that had seen better days to show what can be done. She stretched masking tape along the middle of the car from front bumper to back, then completely detailed one half of the car. She did the same inside the car. Once done, she made a sign for the window telling about her auto detailing service. People could immediately see the results of her work and she developed many new customers by simply driving around.

The SIC code for auto detail services is 7542-03.

Baking service

What will I be doing?

If you have access to a commercial kitchen or oven, you can offer baking services to others. Who? Cake decorators need cakes to decorate. Bakeries need pies or other products baked when their own ovens are busy. Specialty stores without an oven need a place to bake dishes. Caterers need a place to finish preparing some of their foods. Individuals preparing for family feasts and get-togethers need help cooking.

If you enjoy baking and have the equipment and permits (if required), this is a lucrative part-time venture you can run at home.

What will I need to start?

Depending on state and local health codes, you'll probably need a commercial kitchen or oven for this venture. Contact your state or county health department for requirements. If you already have a commercial kitchen or don't need one, you can begin this part-time business by simply letting others know. Customers will want to know what you do, the capacity of your oven, whether you do other preparation, whether you can pick up and deliver and your price.

Who will my customers be?

Your customers will be individuals, cake decorators, coffee houses, restaurants, specialty stores, caterers, sandwich shops, desert shops, ethnic stores and other people and businesses that need to prepare or bake food. Once you've decided what services you will offer, contact potential customers and let them know.

How much should I charge?

Your hourly rate depends on what you're doing. If you need to prepare any food, your rate should be higher than for the time you're waiting for it to bake. So you may have two hourly rates: one for preparation and one for baking.

As an example, baking wedding cakes for a client may require 30 minutes of preparation time at $25 to $40 an hour, plus baking for an hour at $5 to $15 an hour. The baking session would then be priced at $17.50 ($12.50 + $5) to $35 ($20 + $15).

Establish a typical price list for the primary food products you bake.

How much will I make?

Your baking service will build by word-of-mouth advertising and some local publicity, so you won't spend much time marketing. Overhead, including taxes, will take 20 to 50 percent of each dollar you bring in. So a baking service can earn $5,000 to $15,000 in income each year, depending on many factors. Most baking services need some other source of business, such as catering, to pay the costs of maintaining a commercial kitchen.

How can I get started?

Before starting a baking service, talk with potential customers about the need for such a service. This is especially important if you must invest in equipment, licenses and permits. It's not as important if you already have a qualifying kitchen and contacts within the food service industry.

Bicycle repair service

What will I be doing?

Once a major mode of transportation, bicycles are now popular as recreation vehicles. Once tools, now they're toys.

Fortunately, toys also get attention when they're broken. A bicycle repair service maintains, repairs, restores and (sorry for the pun) recycles cycles. If this sounds like fun to you, consider starting your own bicycle repair service from your home or garage.

What will I need to start?

Fixing bikes means you must understand how they work. Although children's bicycles are basic machines, those that adults ride are more sophisticated—and require more knowledge to repair. Unless you have this knowledge or can gain it easily, stay with simpler bikes.

One entrepreneur began a successful bicycle repair service by purchasing children's bikes in any condition. He paid $10 if he could roll them away and $5 if he had to carry them. He then dismantled them, replaced parts as needed from other bikes, painted them and resold them at a profit. Some of the profit went toward attending factory schools for major bicycle brands. Within a few years, his weekend bike recycling service had become a full-time bike shop specializing in racing bikes.

Who will my customers be?

Kids don't buy kids' bikes. Parents and grandparents do. Adults also buy collectors' bikes, mountain bikes, racing bikes and exercise bikes. So your customers will be adults buying for kids or for the kids in themselves. Appeal to both the logic and the emotion of your customers and your business will succeed.

Most bicycle repair services promote themselves with small service ads in local newspapers, on area bulletin boards, in bike shops and through referrals.

How much should I charge?

Although a bicycle repair service sets prices using an hourly rate, the price of most services is quoted to the customer based on the type of job or the value of the results. For example, a shop with a $30-an-hour rate may require 40 minutes to tune up a mountain bike. The price for this service isn't quoted as $30 an hour, but as $20—or $19.95.

Base your pricing on your shop rate, the amount of time required for the typical job and also on the prices of your competitors. Keep your prices lower than those of your competitors if you can until you have too much business, then raise them until you have just the right amount of business to keep you happy.

How much will I make?

No one has ever become rich repairing bicycles. However, many people have started part-time garage ventures that were built into lucrative bicycle businesses. So can you. Initially, you'll spend up to half of your time promoting your business, but that should soon be cut down to 25 percent of your time or less. This is unbillable, but necessary time. Overhead expenses will depend on what type of business you're building, where you're located and how much time you're devoting to it. Figure on keeping 50 to 75 percent of every dollar that comes in the door and you should be accurate.

So 12 hours a week less 25 percent of your time for marketing and administration means 8 billable hours a week. Multiply that by $25 an hour and you have a gross income of $200 a week. You'll probably be able to keep $100 to $150 after expenses. Not Rockefeller, but not bad.

How can I get started?

To start a bicycle repair business, learn as much as you can about bikes and how to repair them. Makes sense. Read the bicycle magazines for additional resources, such as books and associations, that can help you build your business.

The SIC code for bicycle repair services is 7699-74.

Bookkeeping service

What will I be doing?

There are nearly 28,000 full-time bookkeeping services in the U.S., and many more are operated part-time evenings and weekends. Why are there so many? Because records must be kept as money changes hands. A retail store keeps books or records on sales by product, expenses by supplier and wages by employee. These records are used to calculate both profit for the owners and taxes for the government.

If you have skills and training in recordkeeping, you can put them to work keeping records for other businesses, thus building a business of your own. You can operate exclusively or partially out of your home, depending on your needs and those of your customers.

What will I need to start?

To start a bookkeeping service, you will need knowledge and experience in single- and double-entry bookkeeping. It will also be helpful if you know or have access to computer accounting systems. One successful operator furnished each client with a licensed copy of Quicken, a popular check recording system for computers. Once a week she picked up the customer's files on diskette or by modem and developed reports for them.

Setting up a manual bookkeeping system requires only a few supplies, such as journals and ledgers purchased at stationery stores. A computerized bookkeeping system will cost a few thousand dollars to establish. Also consider one of the bookkeeping franchise opportunities advertised in small business magazines.

Who will my customers be?

Your initial customers for a bookkeeping service will be other small businesses. You can work with those in a particular geographic area (shopping mall, suburb, business complex), a trade (gas stations, clothing stores, dentists) or a function (billing, disbursements). As you define your service, you will be defining your customers and how to reach them. Mailings or telephone calls to potential customers in an area or trade can help you build your business.

How much should I charge?

The hourly rate for bookkeeping services is typically $20 to $40. The lower rate will be for low-skill work, such as making entries into a journal or ledger. The higher rate will be for advising clients on solving specific financial problems. You won't be working as a public accountant, but you can still offer useful advice on records. Most bookkeeping services price their work by the month, with a small discount (5 to 10 percent) for annual contracts. If, for example, you specialize in keeping books for contractors, you can set your price by the estimated annual sales. You may also want to add a fee per employee or per subcontractor your client uses.

How much will I make?

Once established, much of your time will be billable to one client or another. Initially, you may spend up to 35 percent of your time marketing your business. Within a few months, this marketing time should be down to 15 to 25 percent. It should never get to 0 percent, as you should always be looking for new customers to replace those that hire a full-time bookkeeper, go out of business or otherwise drop your services. A bookkeeping service with 400 billable hours a year at $30 an hour will have gross sales of $12,000. Allowing 25 percent for overhead gives the owner a net income of $9,000 for the year.

How can I get started?

Before opening your home bookkeeping service, you'll need sufficient training and experience to convince prospects to hire you. If you don't have extensive experience, get some by working for a bookkeeping service. Ethically, you should not go after their customers, but you can use what you've learned about the trade to build your own business. You may even find a service owner who wants to retire in a few years and is willing to sell to you.

Here are a couple of resources:

♦ General Business Services (800-583-9100).

♦ American Institute of Professional Bookkeepers (800-622-0121).

The SIC code for bookkeeping services is 8721-02.

Bridal consultant

What will I be doing?

Weddings are the happiest—and most hectic—times of our lives. As a wedding or bridal consultant, you will be helping brides and parents select wedding supplies and plan services. You will be the calm within the storm. You will plan, organize, order, worry and comfort. If this sounds like fun, consider starting a part-time bridal consultant business.

What will I need to start?

To help brides arrange successful weddings, you must first know what your clients want. You may decide to specialize in ethnic, outdoor, second or even group weddings—managing the many steps required to make the event memorable for your clients. Your skills can be based on reading, but must be tested by experience, either as a volunteer or as an employee in the bridal or wedding industry. There are more than 8,800 bridal shops in the U.S., so you may want to start there, learning and making invaluable contacts.

Who will my customers be?

Customers for your bridal consulting service will be brides, their families and bridal services. In some cases, a bridal shop will hire you to coordinate all services. In other cases, the bride herself will do so. The best way of reaching these potential customers is by participating in local bridal fairs. Also, make sure that wedding shops in your area know of your services and will recommend or hire you.

One successful bridal consultant specialized in helping senior citizen brides. Most customers wanted simple services that involved friends, children and even grandchildren, while focusing on the special needs of the bride.

How much should I charge?

The hourly rate for an established bridal consultant is typically $30 to $60. However, most bridal consultants price their service by the size of the wedding, either as a percentage of the total costs, as a fee per planned guest or a combination of both. For example, a wedding budgeted at $4,000 in services (wedding shop rentals and catering services) may be coordinated by a bridal consultant who charges a fee of 15 to 25 percent ($600 to $1,000) paid by the bride's family and/or the contracted service businesses. A bridal consultant with an hourly rate of $40, for example, would spend 15 to 25 hours planning and coordinating the event (15 to 25 x $40 = $600 to $1,000). With some experience, you can soon develop your own pricing sheet or guidelines to ensure competitive prices for your customers and profit for yourself.

How much will I make?

You will spend 15 to 30 percent of your time marketing your bridal consulting business. As a part-time venture of 12 hours a week, that leaves you about eight to 10 billable hours in a week. An hourly rate of $30 will give you a gross income of $300 a week, and $45 an hour offers $450 a week. Your overhead expenses (advertising, home office, telephone, taxes) will take 20 to 40 percent of your income. The balance is yours.

How can I get started?

Learn your trade. If you don't already have experience working for bridal shops and wedding services, volunteer to help brides coordinate their weddings, charging them nothing other than a letter of recommendation. If there are many competitors in your area, find a specialty that you enjoy. Then let prospective customers know about your services through advertising and publicity.

Also consider joining trade associations, such as the Association of Bridal Consultants (203-355-0464).

The SIC for bridal consultants is 5621-04.

Business plan writer

What will I be doing?

To reach the goal of success in business, you must have a plan. That's true for your weekend home business. It's also true for others who want to start or expand a business. If you have a background or training in business and can write well, consider operating a part-time business plan-writing enterprise from your home.

What will I need to start?

A business plan is simply a written document that summarizes the financial and marketing strategies of a new or existing business. The level of detail required depends on the plan's purpose. Simple business plans help the owners crystallize their ideas into a single document to help them focus efforts. Detailed business plans include cash flow projections, income statements, balance sheets and other documents, as well as specific marketing data.

There are computer software programs that can help you design and write business plans. However, they require a working knowledge of business. The greater the knowledge, the more valuable the plan. To write effective business plans for others, you don't have to know every aspect of their business, but you must understand business principles.

Who will my customers be?

Those starting in business may want only a simple business plan to use as a guidance tool. These are easy to write. Your customers will be those considering a specific business. Other customers will want more complex plans, typically developed for presentation to lenders. A banker or other financial lender doesn't really care what the business is. He or she wants to know how much money is needed, how it will be managed and—most important—how and when it will be paid back with interest.

You can find customers for your business plan services by contacting the Small Business Development Centers in your region. They are in daily contact with people wanting to start or expand a business. Most need help with developing a business plan. You can also find customers by advertising your services in regional business publications. One successful business plan writer found his customers by offering a four-hour seminar on business plans. Some students would write their own, but many saw how much work it was and hired him to write the plan.

How much should I charge?

Business plan writers are typically well-paid. The hourly rate is usually $45 to $75. A simple business plan may require 10 to 20 hours, so is usually priced at $450 to $1,500. A full business plan for a lender may require 40 to 80 hours and be priced at $2,000 to $6,000.

How much will I make?

Working part-time writing business plans is an excellent way to start this home business venture. In many cases, those needing help with startup business plans are working at them evenings and weekends—exactly when you're working. Spending about 25 percent of your time marketing leaves 75 percent of your time as billable. Once established, 12 hours a week can bring you an annual income of $21,000 to $35,000. Overhead, including your home office and taxes, will take the first 25 to 50 percent, but will still leave you with a good income.

How can I get started?

Here are some aids to get you started:

♦ Computer software: BizPlan Builder, Business Plan Toolkit, sold at larger computer stores.

♦ Small Business Development Centers (check local telephone books under Federal Government—Small Business Administration).

Cabinet-refinishing service

What will I be doing?

Not every homeowner who needs kitchen remodeling can afford a complete overhaul. Their needs can be fulfilled more affordably by a cabinet-refinishing service. A cabinet-refinishing service repairs and resurfaces kitchen and bathroom cabinets and countertops in residential and commercial buildings.

The service refinishes or resurfaces cabinets with new paint or other finish, Formica or sheet plastic, hardware, hinges and maybe cabinet doors. Because the existing cabinets are not removed, the cost of refinishing is much lower than replacement.

What will I need to start?

A cabinet-refinishing service requires fewer tools than a cabinet-maker. For most jobs, common hand and some small power tools are enough to do the job. Some training is typically required, but it can be self-taught with your own cabinets and those in friends' homes. A class at a community college or trade school can help you develop the necessary skills. Tools for the job can be purchased for a few hundred dollars or less. Your business may require a contractor's license and bonding. If so, consider this inconvenience a way of developing customer trust.

Who will my customers be?

Your customers for cabinet refinishing include remodeling contractors, homeowners, business owners and property managers. You can contact them in the evenings and do the work over the weekends. You'll find remodeling contractors listed in area telephone books, or can you can buy mailing lists of homeowners in your area. You can even limit the list to those who own homes worth more than $150,000 that are more than 10 years old. A list broker can help.

How much should I charge?

Cabinet refinishing can be difficult work requiring toxic glues and finishes. Make sure you have the proper respiration equipment and coverings. You will be calculating prices using a per-hour rate, but quote the job as a specific fee. The hourly rate for cabinet-refinishing services is typically $35 to $60, priced by the square-foot-surface or running length of the cabinets. Some services charge one rate for replacing countertops and another for refinishing cabinets, calculated by the number of standard doors. Become a customer, calling potential competitors to learn what others charge. If you're working with an experienced and honest remodeling contractor, he or she may help you set your prices.

How much will I make?

Marketing your services will take 15 to 25 percent of your time. So 15 available hours a week will probably give you 12 billable hours. You will use 25 to 50 percent of your income for overhead, depending on who buys materials. At $40 an hour, for example, your potential annual gross income will be nearly $25,000. Knock off a quarter to a half of that for overhead and you know what you can probably earn with a part-time cabinet-refinishing service.

How can I get started?

To get started in this business, learn as much as you can about the process, work for a remodeling contractor if you can to develop experience and contacts and begin gathering your tools. Check into licensing requirements. Finally, begin letting others know through ads or word-of-mouth that your cabinet-refinishing service is ready for new business.

Cake decorator

What will I be doing?

Everyone loves a beautifully decorated cake. Such cakes enhance weddings, birthdays, anniversaries, retirement parties, holidays and other special events. They also offer a good income for those who enjoy decorating cakes.

There are nearly 30,000 full-time cake decorators in the U.S. and many more working part-time from their home. As a cake decorator, you will bake and decorate cakes for weddings and corporate events and functions. If you don't have facilities to bake, you can purchase the cake from a local bakery or from a baking service.

What will I need to start?

To start your cake-decorating service you'll need some experience at the craft. You can train yourself using books available through bakery supply houses and craft stores. You'll also buy cake-decorating equipment and materials from these sources. If you plan to make your own cakes, you may need a professional kitchen, baker's license and baking equipment.

Who will my customers be?

Who will hire you to decorate cakes? Hopefully, many people: wedding consultants, brides and grooms, parents, bakeries, party organizers, individuals and even businesses. The telephone book may yield many of your prospective customers. Also, post information about your service on bulletin boards and consider placing a small ad in the services section of your newspaper.

How much should I charge?

The hourly rate for cake decorators is $25 to $40, depending on what is supplied and the complexity of the design. Some services bake and decorate cakes for $3 to $5 per serving with a minimum charge. Others price by the number of tiers in the cake or by the square inch of the cake's surface. What you charge will depend somewhat on what your competitors charge.

How much will I make?

Once established, your cake-decorating service will sell itself with repeat and referral business. Until then, plan on spending 10 to 20 percent of your time marketing your services to bakeries, bridal consultants, businesses and individuals. Fortunately, a couple hundred dollars in tools and supplies is all you'll need to start, and you'll spend just 10 to 25 percent of your income on overhead expenses. Much of what you make you will keep. How much you actually make depends on how many hours you devote to the business, how well you market your services, how often people recommend you and how well you manage expenses. But if you love what you're doing, you will be well-rewarded.

How can I get started?

To start your cake-decorating business, develop your skills, develop your own unique designs and style, start gathering needed tools and let others know that you are looking for business. Start slow and learn as you go.

The SIC code for cake decorators is 5461-02.

Care giver

What will I be doing?

Health is one of the most important aspects of life. Most people would trade wealth for it. You can be an important part of the health industry while working at home as a care giver.

Care givers provide health care services in their own homes or in their clients' homes. Care may involve simply making sure patients' basic needs are met. Some patients require medications, shots or other services. A few need continual supervision.

What will I need to start?

To start your care giver business, you'll first need a strong desire to serve others. Without it, some of the chores are more difficult. You will also need an understanding of the patient's health problems and how to assist. A degree, certification or advanced courses in nursing will help you.

Typically, special equipment and medications will be provided by others. They may also provide a bed and clothing. What you need to start depends somewhat on the type of care you will provide, whether it's in your home or your patient's, and other factors.

Who will my customers be?

Who hires independent care givers? Insurance companies, hospitals, nursing homes, care management services and individuals (children, parents, other relatives) will be your initial customers. Your ultimate customer will be the patient.

To find customers, let government and private health care organizations in your area know that you are offering in-home care, and inform them of your experience and credentials for doing so.

How much should I charge?

Typically, what you get for health care services will depend on what others are paying. That is, a hospital or insurance company may offer $70 a day per patient for in-home health care. Or a care management service may pay $85 a week for a specific number of visits. Billing will be by the week or month.

How much will I make?

The income you make as a care giver is small, but so are the demands. You can offer care in your home while operating other home businesses. You can have more than one patient at a time. Many people offer quality health care from their homes on a part-time basis to supplement pension or disability payments and allow them to work from home.

How can I get started?

First, check with government health services in your area to learn the requirements for operating a home care business. Some states have stricter laws than others. You may be required to have your home certified. You may also need to take some classes.

Contact Mentor Clinical Care (800-388-5150) for more information.

Carpet-cleaning service

What will I be doing?

There are more than 30,000 full-time carpet-cleaning services in the U.S. and probably twice as many operated as part-time ventures from home. A carpet-cleaning service, as you might expect, cleans carpets and rugs using special equipment. This is typically a home-based business that uses the home as an office, but does the work from a vehicle parked at the customer's location.

What will I need to start?

You can start your carpet-cleaning service with just business cards or fliers passed out to neighbors. Then as you get jobs, rent a carpet-cleaning machine and buy the needed shampoo. As your business grows, you can find used and new professional carpet-cleaning equipment at wholesale janitorial suppliers listed in metropolitan telephone books. They can also suggest cleaning supplies.

Who will my customers be?

Customers for your carpet-cleaning service include individuals, companies and managers of office buildings. Most carpet-cleaning services specialize in specific customers, focusing marketing on homes, office complexes, retail stores, shopping malls, government offices or other groups. If your business is located in a large city and you have many competitors, you will specialize more than if your business serves a town of 10,000.

You can reach your customers through mailing lists, fliers, small service ads in newspapers and advertisements in the yellow pages of area phone books.

How much should I charge?

You will calculate the prices of your services using an hourly rate, typically $25 to $50. However, you will quote the customer prices based on the size of the carpet cleaned and the need for cleaning. That is, you may charge 15 to 25 cents a square foot, with the lower price for light cleaning and the higher price for carpets needing more work to clean.

Many carpet-cleaning services make pricing easier for the customer by quoting by the room. A 10 x 12 foot room of 120 square feet will range from $18 to $30 at 15 to 25 cents a square foot, so the room rate can be quoted at $17.95 to $29.95 and require about a half hour to clean. Most per-room rates require a minimum number of rooms, typically three, to reduce the time lost to setting up and taking down equipment at a site. In addition, some carpet-cleaning services add a specific price per room for moving furniture to clean the carpet.

How much will I make?

Initially, you'll spend up to half of your time marketing your business. But you will soon reduce that to 15 to 25 percent of your time through repeat and referral business. Overhead expenses will range from 20 to 40 percent of every dollar you take in, depending on the value of your equipment and how much you spend on marketing your services. A part-time carpet-cleaning service can earn $15 to $25 net per hour if it is dedicated to the business.

How can I get started?

You can learn the skills required for efficiently cleaning carpets by working for a carpet-cleaning or janitorial service. Doing so, you will also learn what equipment and supplies to use. If you maintain a good relationship with your employer, he or she may even help you establish your noncompeting business and give or sell you accounts.

Resources include:

♦ Carpet and Rug Cleaning Institute (706-278-3176).

♦ Franchises: Rug Doctor (800-678-7844), Von Schrader Co. (800-626-6916), Chem-Dry Carpet Cleaning (800-841-6583).

The SIC code for carpet-cleaning services is 7217-04.

Cart/kiosk sales

What will I be doing?

Peddlers have been selling their wares from carts for hundreds of years. You too can sell food, novelties, flowers and other impulse products using either movable carts or stationary booths or kiosks (pronounced: KEY-osks).

What will I need to start?

Location is an important part of starting a cart/kiosk business. A poor location will bring few customers and little sales. Fortunately, it's easier to move a cart or kiosk to a new location that to move a retail store or restaurant. But you can't just set up your cart anywhere you want. You will probably need a city or county permit, as well as permission from the owners of the property where you place your mini-business. Depending on what and how you sell, you may also need lighting, signage, a cash register, inventory, a cart or kiosk (you can rent these) and a knowledge of people and what they want.

Who will my customers be?

Your customers will be those who want to buy specific products or services at a location convenient to them. This could be almost anything, anywhere. One successful part-time cart operator sold hot dogs and sausages from a steam cart that he kept in the corner of a warehouse. Just before lunchtime he would roll it to his regular location, start it up and begin serving. Customers came to him.

Your cart or kiosk must be located where customers are, such as on a busy city street or in a shopping mall. You can operate your business part-time or full-time, year-round or seasonally. By watching when and where you make sales, you can determine the best location and times for your business.

How much should I charge?

You will be charging by the product or service you sell, but should calculate your time at $20 to $40 an hour, depending on the cost of your equipment and its operation. Many cart and kiosk operators use a simple multiplier to mark up products to their retail price. Food carts usually mark prices up 300 to 400 percent of wholesale. For example, a 30-cent hot dog, 10-cent bun and 10 cents in condiments costs 50 cents in materials and sells for $1.50 to $2. Products sold from a cart or kiosk are typically marked up 200 to 300 percent from wholesale. A $4 wholesale necklace is sold at $8 to $12—or $7.99 to $11.99. The markup is less because no product preparation is required.

How much will I make?

How much you make with your cart or kiosk depends on many factors, the greatest of which is the location. If you get to keep 50 cents of every dollar you take in (after all expenses), a cart that sells an average of $100 an hour (a hot dog a minute!) will give you $50 for the hour. A kiosk with an average income of $35 an hour over the day will give you $17.50 an hour.

Some carts and kiosks pay a percentage rent to the owner of their location. The typical rate is 10 to 20 percent. A jewelry cart that sells $600 in merchandise a day will be paying $60 to $120 for the day's rent.

How can I get started?

To start your cart or kiosk business, first do some market research. Look around your community for successful cart operators and study them. A few hours or days of study will help you estimate their income, expenses and profits. Buy something from them to learn more. Pick a slow time and they may talk with you about their business.

Next, pick a product. It must be something that will sell well, but isn't already oversold at your location.

Finally, find the best location. Add a cart or kiosk, some products or services and have fun.

Here are some sources for carts and kiosks:

- ◆ Westrock Vending Vehicles (516-666-5252).
- ◆ The Great Gazebo (517-332-6126).

Catering service

What will I be doing?

Catering is a popular business with more than 43,000 businesses catering in the U.S. What does a caterer do? He or she purchases, prepares, delivers and serves food for special events. If you enjoy preparing food and making others happy, a catering service may be a good home-based business for you.

What will I need to start?

First, you'll need to check with local and state health departments to determine what licenses, permits and certification are required to operate a catering service. If you prepare your own food, your kitchen will probably need to be certified as a commercial kitchen. Some caterers work around this by renting restaurant kitchens during the slow midmorning and midafternoon periods.

You'll also need utensils and delivery and service tools, as well as a source of food and supplies. If you're renting a commercial kitchen, some of these requirements will be available there.

Who will my customers be?

Customers for your catering service include individuals giving parties, companies needing to feed employees at sales meetings or picnics, and groups and associations conducting meetings or seminars.

One successful caterer began her business as an employee of a popular restaurant. She contracted with the owners to pay them 25 percent of her business if she could use the kitchen during her off-hours. With careful planning, both profited from the partnership.

How much should I charge?

The hourly rate for catering services is typically $25 to $75, depending on many factors. The greater the caterer's skills and reputation, the higher the hourly rate. Pricing of catered events is typically by person. A catered company picnic may be priced at $6 per person, while a formal dinner may be priced at $45 per person. The caterer's hourly rate is added to the costs of food and preparation to establish the base price.

How much will I make?

Your catering service can be very profitable once you've learned how to operate it efficiently. Waste is the greatest enemy in the food service industry. Lower the waste and you will increase profits.

One successful caterer specialized in catering weddings, planning one on each day of the weekend. She charged $8 per person with a 50-person minimum. After paying for food, preparation, delivery and service, she earned about $22 an hour for her time. The 14 hours she spent on her business each weekend netted her about $16,000 a year—after taxes!

How can I get started?

Read the book *Catering: Start and Run a Money-Making Business* by Judy Richards (TAB/McGraw-Hill).

The SIC code for catering services is 5812-12.

Childcare

What will I be doing?

With a childcare service you provide care, entertainment and meals or snacks for children in either your home or the children's homes.

There are more than 55,000 full-time childcare centers in the U.S. and many more individuals who care for one or two children in their home or baby-sit at the children's homes.

Although the income per child is moderate, caring for more than one child at a time can help you make a good living from your home.

What will I need to start?

To care for children you must really care about them. If you have experience and/or training in child development, you're off to a good start. You'll also need to have a home that is child-friendly, as well as accessible to parents who need to drop off their children. Your childcare business may also require licensing, inspection and certification, depending on local regulations. If you prepare food and serve it to children, you may need additional licensing or certification. Of course, you'll also need things to entertain and train children.

Who will my customers be?

Your customers will be parents and grandparents of young children. You may also decide to offer your services to local businesses, who will then offer it to their employees. To reach potential customers, let your friends and neighbors know about your new business. Contact local schools, place a small service ad in the newspaper and publicize your business locally.

How much should I charge?

You will price your childcare services by the hour and the service provided. That is, you may charge $2 an hour for four or more hours a day, $2.50 an hour for less than four hours a day and an additional $3 per meal. You will then add these prices up to give customers a single price, such as $105 a week for five nine-hour days, including meals.

How much will I make?

Most of what you make with your childcare service you will get to keep. Overhead expenses include toys, meals and incidentals. The greatest expense is already paid: the cost of your home. In fact, you will be able to deduct the cost of the part of your home used for childcare. Use *Form 8829*, Expenses for Business Use of Your Home, which includes a special calculation for day-care facilities.

How can I get started?

Start by learning about local requirements. Check with state and local government offices to find out about regulations regarding child care. Next, plan your business, how you will operate it and how much you will charge. Finally, let others know about it: advertise, promote, tell.

Contact the National Association for Family Child Care (800-359-3817) for additional advice.

The SIC code for child care services is 8351-01.

Chimney sweep

What will I be doing?

A chimney sweep service cleans the soot and other byproducts of fuel-burning heat systems from residential and commercial chimneys. The job of cleaning chimneys, if done right, isn't as dirty as imagined. However, it typically requires that you climb up on roofs to operate the cleaning equipment. If heights bother you or you have physical limitations, consider another business.

There are more than 4,500 full-time chimney sweep services in the U.S. and thousands more working part-time. The chimney sweep business is busiest in the fall and winter, and less busy in the spring and summer. This is a good opportunity for those with jobs or other home businesses that are busiest in the spring and summer. The income is good, because it is a job that many people can't or don't want to do themselves.

What will I need to start?

Chimney cleaning isn't rocket science. However, it does require a working knowledge of how to efficiently clean chimneys without dirtying your customer's home or office. If you don't have experience in this task, find books that explain the process and the needed tools. Ask your librarian.

You can also learn about chimney sweeps by hiring one. If your home doesn't have a chimney or you live in an apartment, hire one for a friend who has a chimney and watch the sweep at work.

Who will my customers be?

Who will hire you to clean or sweep their chimneys, fireplaces and furnace stacks? Your customers will be homeowners, business owners, apartment building owners and commercial building owners. You may decide to specialize in one type or another, or you may even expand your business to include selling heating system components.

To find your customers, first identify who they are, where they probably live and what they need. Then go after them as best you can: advertise, hand out fliers and contact local fireplace shops and heating system suppliers.

How much should I charge?

The hourly rate for a chimney sweep service, including labor and overhead costs, is typically $25 to $50. However, most sweeps price their services by the job. They may charge by the number of flues, their length and size, the amount of time since the last cleaning and other factors. If your business is just starting out, consider pricing your service lower than that of your competitors to develop business. Once you're established and have a reputation for good work and service, you can increase your prices accordingly.

How much will I make?

Initially, up to a third of your time will be spent marketing your business. As your sweep business grows, more of your time will be billable. If your time is limited, a spouse or friend can help you by handling the marketing and scheduling while you do the jobs.

About 60 to 80 percent of everything you make will be yours to keep. The 20 to 40 percent of expenses will cover tools, transportation to and from jobs, home office expenses, taxes and other necessities of business.

How can I get started?

To start your chimney sweep business, first learn your trade by reading and watching or, even better, by working for a chimney sweep service. Working for others can help you determine whether this is the right business for you, while it helps you develop efficient skills that can make you more money.

The SIC code for chimney sweep services is 7349-16.

Clown/entertainer/magician

What will I be doing?

Does entertaining others, clowning around or doing magic tricks sound like a fun way to make money in your spare time? It can be.

Entertaining others with magic, humor, music or other talents is an age-old profession. As an entertainer you will be developing an act that makes people laugh, wonder and think. You will distract them from everyday cares and help them discover the joy in life.

There really aren't enough clowns in the world. In fact, less than a thousand clowns advertise their services in the telephone books of the

U.S. Nearly 8,000 entertainers and more than a thousand magicians promote themselves in the phone books.

What will I need to start?

Entertaining doesn't really require talent. What separates good entertainers from great ones is talent, but it isn't a necessary ingredient. Like other crafts, entertaining can be taught and learned. If you learn all you can about the business, practice and prepare, you too can succeed as a part-time entertainer.

Who will my customers be?

Who needs your service as an entertainer? Practically everybody. However, because there is "free" entertainment on television, few people are willing to pay you. Those who do are parents, businesses, bars and restaurants and entertainment companies, such as comedy clubs.

How much should I charge?

Once you've made a name for yourself, your skills as an entertainer may earn you a good income. Until then, plan on "paying your dues."

The hourly rate for an entertainer ranges from $20 to $35 and includes some preparation time. However, most entertainers charge by the event, depending on expected length. For example, a clown for birthday parties may charge $60 for appearing at a child's party, which includes 45 minutes of makeup and travel time, an hour entertaining at the party and about $8 worth of token prizes and balloons.

How much will I make?

Once established, at least three-quarters of your time will be billable. The other 25 percent of your time will be spent talking to people on the telephone and scheduling events. Overhead costs are minimal, depending on the costs of your equipment. A magician can invest $100 or $1,000 in equipment. The magician's rate should change accordingly.

Part-time entertainers who do four shows a week can expect to pocket $150 to $500, depending on the length and complexity of the shows and the expenses needed to put them on.

How can I get started?

Entertaining others is a learned skill—actually many skills. It's not just getting up in front of an audience. Entertaining people begins by developing an act, writing jokes, practicing tricks, designing makeup and selecting props. There are clown schools and magic schools, but most part-time entertainers learn their trade on their own with books and experience.

Even clowns have an SIC code: 7929-07. The code for entertainers is 7929-03 and for magicians, 7929-04.

Collection service

What will I be doing?

Most people pay their bills on time. When they don't, a collection service may be hired. Collection services assist businesses in collecting money owed to them by their customers, while encouraging a continuing relationship.

Many of the people who operate successful collection services aren't those with pristine credit themselves. In fact, many have had debt problems in the past and know how to help others get out of debt. They offer a useful service to both businesses and consumers. They also get paid well for their service.

What will I need to start?

To start your own collection service you'll first need an understanding of the credit and collection side of business. Books will help, but practical experience in either or both sides of credit will give you an edge. You'll need "thick skin," respect for yourself and for your clients and honesty. You will also need a telephone and some office supplies. This is a venture that can be operated evenings, weekends or nearly any time.

You don't have to be a lawyer, but you will have to learn about the laws of credit and collection. There are many books and pamphlets available on what you can and cannot do as a collection service.

Who will my customers be?

Who will hire your collection service? Businesses with overdue accounts receivable will need you to help them collect. In most cases, the businesses have already tried unsuccessfully to collect on the accounts. By the time you get an account, there may be bad feelings on both sides or your client's customer may have thought the bill was canceled. Your customers will be businesses, but without their customers—those who owe money—you won't be paid.

Some collection services specialize in health care, child support, small business, retail credit or other areas. If you have special knowledge or experience in one of these areas, you may be able to collect bad debts where others can't. This is a good selling point to your customers.

How much should I charge?

Most collection services don't get paid by the hour. (If they do, the range is $30 to $60, depending on the type and size of debts and the success of the collector.) Usually, if you don't collect, you don't get paid.

How much should you charge for your collection services? The typical range is 25 to 50 percent of the value of the debt. A collection service that gets the debtor to pay a $1,000 medical bill will earn $250 to $500, depending on the age of the bill and the agreement with the business. Most debts are for a few hundred dollars. Some collection services don't use the telephone, but rely on legal-sounding letters to collect.

How much will I make?

Income from a collection service depends on your skills to find collectible debts and get them paid. So income can range from $0 to $1,000 a week. Within a few months you'll learn whether this is a business you will enjoy and profit from.

How can I get started?

Consider starting your business with a single business account and a specific group of debts to test your skills and interests. Then expand as you wish. If you have credit and collection experience, your learning curve will be shorter and your profits will come faster than without this valuable experience.

Most important, remember that the service you provide is valuable to both your customers and theirs.

Contact the American Collectors' Association (612-926-6547) for more information.

Commercial artist/graphic designer

What will I be doing?

Do you love to draw and paint? If so, you may have the desire and skills to sell your services as a freelance commercial artist or graphic designer. As such, you will draw or design brochures, sales literature, company logos, unique signs, banners, certificates and a wide variety of other artistic products for businesses.

What will I need to start?

Besides training in art and graphics, you'll need the tools of your trade: design and drawing equipment and supplies. You'll also need knowledge about how art is applied to commerce. Look around you at the advertising world to see striking examples of beauty and purpose in commercial art.

Within your home you can establish a work studio and a small office. If you don't have much space, consider a desk that can serve both purposes.

Who will my customers be?

Most commercial art and graphic designs are sold to businesses and advertising agencies. They are usually commissioned based on samples included in your portfolio. So develop a representative folio of samples and get appointments to show them to potential customers.

How much should I charge?

Commercial artists and graphic designers have a broad hourly rate, depending on skills, experience and the commercial value of the end product. The hourly rate will range from $30 to $90 or more. The product, however, will be priced by the size and complexity of the job. For example, designing a four-page brochure may require about nine hours at an hourly rate of $45, but the price will be quoted to the customer as $4,000. To justify your price, ask the value of the entire project and quote your price as a percentage of that total value. Your fee may be less than 5 percent of the total value of a specific advertising campaign.

How much will I make?

About 25 percent of your time will be devoted to marketing once you get your business moving. Until then, as much as two-thirds of your time will be marketing time. Overhead expenses for a home studio and office will average 20 to 40 percent, depending on equipment and efficiency. You can earn $10,000 to $30,000 or more a year with a part-time commercial art or graphic design service.

How can I get started?

If you're already an artist, learn as much as you can about how art is successfully used in business and commerce. Learn about collateral and proofs. Work for a commercial artist or graphic design service to develop your skills and knowledge. Study your potential competitors. Begin developing contacts within your trade. Find a specialty where you have little or no competition.

The SIC code for commercial artists and graphic designers is 7336-04.

Companion to the elderly

What will I be doing?

Everybody needs a friend. If you enjoy helping others, especially older people, you can establish a home business as a companion and health assistant to elderly or disabled people. You can operate this business from your home, by visiting clients at their homes or by telephone.

What will I need to start?

Many customers will hire you not for health reasons, but for social ones. They may need someone to talk to or to listen to them. They may need help writing letters and paying bills or remembering to take medication. To start your business you will need patience, compassion and a good ear. You may also need transportation to and from your clients' homes. You should have some experience with the elderly, such as having an elderly parent or grandparent or volunteering at a nursing or retirement home.

Who will my customers be?

Your customers will be the elderly, children of the elderly, social services and health organizations. Or you may be hired by a nursing home to make regular visits to individual guests.

To find customers, check the local telephone book for government social services for the elderly. A few telephone calls and a visit will tell you what services are now available and how you can fit in. You may also get referrals.

How much should I charge?

The profit in this work is small financially and large socially. Your fees will be based on an hourly rate of $15 to $25, depending on the number of patients, location and your unbillable time. Most companion services work to establish clients that live close to each other, such as in a retirement community or older neighborhood, to reduce commuting time and increase referral business. With efficiency, a companion can spend two half-hour or four 15-minute sessions a month with a client for less than $30 a month. For some clients, that will be a lot of money. But if you can help them with cleaning or paying bills, the value to them will be greater than your cost.

How much will I make?

A part-time companion service can earn $100 to $200 a week, working just one day on the weekend or a couple of evenings each week. You won't get rich financially, but you will be giving others much-needed friendship.

How can I get started?

Practice on elderly or disabled friends. Visit them regularly to determine what they need, how often and when. Once you've decided to start the business, ask for referrals.

Computer instructor

What will I be doing?

Computers are everywhere: businesses, homes, schools, government. Technology has grown so fast that many people are afraid of computers because they don't understand them. If you do, maybe you can start a home-based computer instruction business.

A computer instructor teaches users how to get the most from their computers. You don't have to be an expert or a programmer, just a teacher. You need to know more about computers than your students and be able to transfer that knowledge.

What will I need to start?

You don't need a computer to start this part-time business, because you can rent classrooms with computers already in them. The main thing you need is knowledge. You must understand how computers (hardware) and programs (software) work together to accomplish specific tasks. To gain this knowledge, read, practice, take a class, read some more, practice some more.

For example, as many people were intimidated by the introduction of the Windows 95 operating system, one enterprising man set up a two-hour class that helped people become comfortable with it. He learned enough to teach the class by reading computer magazines, buying some books and videos on the subject and spending some time at the computer learning about the system. He then offered his class to businesses, individuals at high school computer labs and colleges— anywhere that had computers. He charged $20 a student and typically trained at least 10 students each evening.

Who will my customers be?

Your customers for computer instruction will be both individuals and companies. You will earn more by instructing large groups, because even though the fee-per-student is smaller, the total income per hour is greater with groups.

Computer instructors typically design classes around popular programs or applications, then give fliers promoting the classes to businesses and individuals. Every few weeks, the fliers are revised with new class dates.

Once you have a student for a class, make sure he or she is on your mailing list to receive information on advanced classes.

How much should I charge?

The hourly rate for computer instructors is typically $35 to $75, depending on the knowledge required and the number of students. That is, 10 students would each be paying $3.50 to $7.50 an hour for your class.

Most computer instruction is priced by the class session or group of sessions. That is, a three-hour evening class may be priced at $15 per student. Other instructors offer a series of progressive classes with an easy-payment plan. Find out what your competitors charge and how you can offer more for less.

How much will I make?

About two-thirds of your time as a computer instructor will be spent instructing. The balance of your time will be used marketing your services, learning more about your subject and setting up classes. A part-time business can earn $200 to $300 a week. Depending on how you price your services and to whom you teach, your overhead expenses (classes, equipment, programs, office supplies, telephone, taxes) will range from 20 to 40 percent of your income.

How can I get started?

Training is available for those who want to be computer instructors. Of course, the training is available via computer. One excellent resource is Computer Training Forum (GO DPTRAIN), available through CompuServe online service.

The SIC code for computer instructors is 8243-01.

Computer maintenance service

What will I be doing?

Computers are wonders of electronics. Yet, like other contraptions, they sometimes fail. If you know how to fix them or know how to find resources to fix them, you can earn a very good income doing so from your home.

A computer maintenance service, as you might expect, maintains and repairs computers at the customer's site or at home. Related services are also offered by computer maintenance services. A remote backup service uses telephone lines and modems to make backup copies of information stored on customer's computers. A remote maintenance service diagnoses and repairs customer's software problems using telephone lines and modems.

What will I need to start?

To maintain and repair computers, you'll need to know how they work and what to do when they don't. Classes and books can help. You'll also need hardware tools and diagnostic tools. Hardware tools will help you open up a computer and replace components. Diagnostic tools are software programs that can help you identify problems and solutions.

Upgrading and Repairing PCs by Scott Mueller (Que) is a 1,400-page book with information on nearly all aspects of computer maintenance and repair, including technical reference. It's available at larger bookstores and from some computer stores. It is one of the "secrets" that computer maintenance services have.

Who will my customers be?

Customers for your computer maintenance service include companies that don't have their own computer maintenance people. Individuals will also be your customers, but the more lucrative market is working with businesses that have more than one computer and use them to make a profit. They need and are more willing to pay for computer maintenance and repair.

One way to find customers for your service is to offer free diagnostics and troubleshooting. There are software programs that will help you find problems and resolve conflicts on PCs. Offering this service to select prospects may turn them into customers as they learn how valuable you can be to them.

Also consider working on-call for computer stores to back up their repair service. If they don't have one, contract your service to them.

How much should I charge?

Computer maintenance typically earns an hourly rate of $35 to $75, depending on what's done and how efficiently it is completed. Most computer maintenance is priced by the task, such as backing up or copying system files, or priced by the Mb (megabyte) of storage.

The hourly rate for computer repair is higher, because the knowledge, skills and tools are more valuable. A computer repair service will usually charge $50 to $100 an hour for repair. Because the time to repair a computer problem is difficult to estimate, most repair services charge by the hour.

How much will I make?

A part-time computer maintenance service can typically bill about 400 hours a year, once established. At $40 an hour, the gross income is $16,000, with about 60 to 75 percent of that going into the owner's pocket. It's one of the more lucrative home businesses available.

How can I get started?

First, learn your craft through books, classes, videos and hands-on experience. Many computer maintenance services develop experience as employees, then move on as independent contractors.

Begin gathering your tools, and then start looking for customers. You may specialize in maintaining Windows NT, Novell or LANtastic networks, or you may prefer to stick to maintaining single or stand-alone PCs. If competition is high for general services, you may specialize in servicing printers or voice mail systems or other components. Find a need and fill it.

For more information, contact the Independent Computer Consultants' Association (314-997-4633).

The SIC code for computer maintenance services is 7378-01.

Construction cleanup service

What will I be doing?

If you want to be paid to exercise on the weekends, consider starting your own construction cleanup service.

Residential and commercial buildings under construction are a mess. Carpenters, electricians, plumbers and other subcontractors build fast and efficient, throwing waste aside for someone else to clean up. You can offer to clean up the site for an hourly rate, a flat fee based on the size of the building or for a reduced rate if you can recycle waste.

Specifically, construction cleanup services pick up trim and waste from excavation, drywall, electrical, plumbing, roofing and other contractors. They do so evenings or on weekends when construction workers aren't on-site.

What will I need to start?

Construction cleanup, obviously, doesn't require extensive skills or training. The work is physically demanding and does require that you learn to work efficiently. Also, the owners and contractors are trusting you to pick up only waste and not good materials. Develop this trust into a relationship of honesty and your business will grow.

You will need safety equipment to ensure that you don't step on nails or are injured by other materials. You will probably need to be licensed and bonded as are other subcontractors. You may need a truck to haul away materials, though some services keep a large dumpster at the site where materials can be placed during cleanup.

Who will my customers be?

Your customers for a construction cleanup service are building contractors and subcontractors. You may work directly with a general contractor responsible for a group or subdivision of homes or a large commercial building. Or you may be hired by electrical or plumbing contractors to clean up after their crews and recycle what you can. Check your area telephone books for contractors.

One enterprising construction cleanup service also rented outdoor toilets to construction sites. Not only did it add to income, it also gave the cleanup business a prominent place to advertise their services.

How much should I charge?

The hourly rate for a construction cleanup service is $20 to $45. However, the service is usually priced by the size of the job, measured in square feet, and the difficulty. For example, you may be hired to clean up a new home of 2,000 square feet every weekend for four weekends. If you calculate that the total time will be about six hours and you charge $25 an hour, your fee will be $150. Divide that amount by the square footage and you come up with 7.5 cents a square foot. If you find that your time estimate was accurate, you can bid future jobs at 5 cents a square foot for easy jobs and 10 cents a square foot for difficult jobs, with the average rate at 7.5 cents a square foot.

How much will I make?

Once you've established your business and developed some experience, most of your time will be spent working rather than selling your services. In fact, you may ask someone in your family to take calls, quote jobs and schedule your time. If so, you can be more productive and more profitable. Remember to deduct for overhead, including a pickup truck or a car and utility trailer, as needed.

How can I get started?

Do you know any contractors? If so, talk with them about your service, offering to do one job for free if they will show you what to do and give you a reference when done. If you don't know any contractors, call a few and offer your services. After you've done a couple of jobs, produce a flier listing your services, references and prices, then circulate it at job sites and mail it to contractors.

Don't forget to check with state and local construction licensing offices, because your area may require licensing, bonding, certification or other regulations for your service.

Cooking instructor

What will I be doing?

Cooking can be either fun or work. If it's fun to you, consider teaching others how to make it fun for them. Become a cooking instructor, offering classes in your home, in your clients' homes or other locations.

A cooking instructor teaches others how to prepare, cook and serve food. Some cooking instructors teach general cooking techniques, but most specialize in a particular type of cuisine: ethnic, quick and easy, party, commercial, vegetarian, etc.

What will I need to start?

To become a cooking instructor you'll need to develop your cooking skills, as well as your teaching methods. Most cooking instructors develop their own set of tips and suggestions that make food preparation easier, faster, more tasty or more eye-pleasing. Review your own knowledge of cooking and come up with a dozen or so tips you could pass on to others. What techniques have you learned that you wish you knew when you started cooking?

One cook who taught herself to cook from a wheelchair is teaching others to do the same. Her home has a few special aids in the kitchen, but most of what she teaches are tips and techniques for using a standard kitchen.

Who will my customers be?

Most of your customers will be individuals or small groups in a seminar. Reach them through newspaper advertisements and publicity. Tell local newspapers about your unique service and you may get a write-up in the feature section. If so, make copies of the article and give it to potential customers.

If you have extensive experience as a professional cook, you can train other professionals in your advanced techniques or your cuisine. Contact potential customers through restaurants and culinary unions.

How much should I charge?

There is a wide range of hourly rates for cooking instructors, depending on the skills taught and whether those skills will be used for commercial or recreational cooking. A professional cook will benefit more and pay more than someone who cooks for a family. The typical hourly rate is $30 to $75. However, most instructors charge by the class, with the fee depending on the amount of time, the cost of the classroom and ingredients and the size of the class.

How much will I make?

Your cooking instruction will soon sell itself, developing referral business for you. Until then, plan to spend 10 to 30 percent of your time promoting your service. How much of each dollar of income you will be able to keep depends on your overhead, such as kitchen or classroom rental, ingredients, advertising costs, taxes, etc. Expect overhead costs of 20 to 30 percent, excluding your kitchen and ingredients which add another 10 to 20 percent to your expenses.

How can I get started?

To sell your skills and knowledge, you must first have lots of them to go around. Learn your craft. Look for useful techniques. Discover what makes cooking enjoyable for you. Find out who might be willing to pay you for this knowledge. Test your ideas on others.

The SIC code for cooking instructors is 8299-24.

Crafts business

What will I be doing?

If you enjoy making crafts for yourself and as gifts, you may also be able to sell them.

That idea has occurred to thousands of people, it seems, as you visit craft shows where everything imaginable is made and sold. So how can *you* profitably sell your crafts? You can either find a better product or a better market.

What will I need to start?

To start a successful crafts business you'll first need a craft product that people want more than they want the money it costs to buy. Trivets and pot holders don't sell well because most people can find them at discount stores. Your craft has to be more unique. Cow dolls were unique for awhile, and sold well. Today, there are so many that the discount stores sell them. Keep watching craft magazines, talk with experienced crafters and ask people what crafts they buy. Knowing what sells is a good place to start your crafts business.

You'll also need tools, materials, equipment, supplies and other things, all depending on what it is you will be making.

Who will my customers be?

Crafts are typically sold to individuals by you or by someone selling for you. You can sell direct to friends and neighbors or at craft shows. Those who might sell for you include wholesalers, retailers and sales representatives.

How can you find out what shows are in your area? Ask other crafters, ask at local craft supply stores, watch local newspapers, contact area chambers of commerce and subscribe to craft magazines that list regional shows. *Sunshine Artists U.S.A.* magazine (800-597-2573) lists hundreds of announcements each month.

How much should I charge?

The hourly rate for making and selling crafts depends on the craft, your skills and the market. The rate can range from $25 to $75 an hour. I include studio rates and pricing for specific crafts in my book, *The Crafter's Guide to Pricing Your Work* (Betterway Books).

How much will I make?

Your crafts business will require about 75 percent of your time making items and the rest selling them. Expect to spend more time selling until the business is established, then as your reputation grows, even less time. Your overhead costs depend on what you're making and what tools and materials it takes to produce your crafts. The range is 20 to 40 percent overhead.

A key to profitable crafts is productivity. That is, you must be efficient at your craft, wasting little time or effort as you make your product. It's okay to work at a more leisurely pace, but remember that if you rent a studio by the hour, it will cost less the quicker you work. Also, the more you produce, the more you can sell.

How can I get started?

Learn everything you can about your craft, who needs it, why they buy it, how much they usually pay and who else is selling what you're making. You may already know the answers. If not, spend some time getting them.

Make some samples, show them to others, take some to a crafts show to test and begin the learning process. You will soon learn what works and what doesn't.

Desktop publisher

What will I be doing?

Computers have revolutionized many businesses, including the publishing business. A growing field is that of computer-aided or desktop publishing (DTP). With the help of computers, thousands of people are starting part- and full-time businesses in their homes to design and produce printed materials.

Computers are used to produce fliers, brochures, slim jims (narrow brochures), letterheads, envelopes, business cards, community newspapers, commercial newsletters and many other creative products.

What will I need to start?

Desktop publishing requires skills and knowledge in the areas of design, computers, colors, business documents and writing and editing. For equipment, you'll need a computer, desktop publishing software, a printer and some supplies. DTP software includes a page design program (Aldus Pagemaker, Microsoft Publisher, Corel Ventura) and/or a word processing program (Microsoft Word, Corel WordPerfect, Lotus Word Pro) and some drawing programs (Adobe Illustrator, Corel Draw, Paintbrush).

Who will my customers be?

Customers for your desktop publishing service include businesses, associations and individuals. DTP services in smaller towns offer a wide variety of documents designed on computers, while those in larger cities tend to specialize. One service may specialize in producing association newsletters, while another offers small business startup sets that include letterheads, envelopes, business cards and brochures or fliers for a set price.

How can you reach your customers? The best way is usually to develop your own creative business documents using your DTP skills and system, then mail them to prospective customers. You may also want to place a small service ad in the business section of your local newspaper.

How much should I charge?

The hourly rate for a desktop publishing service varies greatly with the value of the product you produce and your efficiency. Typically, the hourly rate for DTP services is $35 to $75, but most jobs are priced by the product. You can calculate the amount of time required to produce your documents, or you can rely on DTP pricing books, such as Robert Brenner's *Pricing Guide for Desktop Publishing Services* (Brenner Information Group, 619-538-0093).

How much will I make?

Most desktop publishing services require 30 to 50 percent of their time to market their services. This means that 50 to 70 percent of their time is billable. Overhead expenses (a computer system and software, supplies, telephone, taxes) take 20 to 40 percent off the top of what you make. So a part-time desktop publisher working 16 hours a week at a shop rate of $40 an hour will gross about $384 (16 x 40 x 60) and net $230 to $307, depending on overhead.

How can I get started?

You can start your desktop publishing service by learning more about the trade, the opportunities and the costs. Read my book, *Upstart Guide to Owning and Managing a Desktop Publishing Service* (Upstart Publishing). Also consider joining the National Association of Desktop Publishers (508-887-7900).

The SIC code for desktop publishing services is 5734-03.

Disc jockey (DJ) service

What will I be doing?

Nearly everyone likes music. It's especially popular for parties, weddings and other social get-togethers. You can be at the center of the music and fun with a DJ service, providing music and entertainment for parties and events.

What will I need to start?

You don't have to be a musician or work at a radio station to start a DJ service. But you do need to love music. You may decide to specialize in a type of music or audience or you may want to offer a variety of music.

Most DJ services use a professional sound control board, microphone, CD players, tape players and a speaker system. They can be purchased for a few thousand dollars or rented from a local radio station that has such equipment for remote broadcasts.

You must also have a knowledge of your audience's musical tastes. That is, you wouldn't play heavy metal at a religious wedding reception. Find out who will be there and what types of music they like, and then play to your audience.

Who will my customers be?

Customers for your disc jockey service include individuals, groups and businesses. In the same week, you may be asked to provide music and entertainment for a wedding, a country dance and a company office party. You may also work one evening a week replacing the house band at a fraternal lodge.

To reach these potential customers, first develop a flier or brochure that tells what you do and how much it costs. Then give the flier to everyone you know and ask for referrals. If you work at a local radio station, ask for an employee discount on radio "spots" or commercials advertising your DJ service.

How much should I charge?

The hourly rate for a disc jockey service depends on the equipment, your entertainment skills and your popularity. Your hourly rate as you begin will be lower than what it will be once you have a year's experience. The typical hourly rate for a disc jockey service is $24 to $60. If you play at functions where alcohol is consumed, you may want to include an extra fee for handling people who celebrate too much.

Most DJ events typically require a half hour to an hour for setup and takedown of equipment. Whether you build this time into your hourly rate or add time to the session, it should be part of your package price. For example, a four-hour dance may require an extra hour, making it a five-hour gig. If your rate is $30 an hour, your package price for a four-hour dance is $150.

How much will I make?

Most of your time as a disc jockey service will be billable to a customer. Expect to spend about 20 percent of your time marketing once your business is established. Until then, spend half of your time selling your services. Overhead expenses depend on whether you own your sound equipment or rent it, as well as its value. DJ services that play two events a weekend can make $200 to $400 a week in extra cash.

How can I get started?

To start your DJ service, first study the competition: other DJ services, entertainers, bands, etc. To begin, you may have to compete on price. Once established, your name value will bring you a higher price. You can also learn your trade and promote yourself as a weekend disc jockey at a local radio station. You will be paid close to minimum wage, but the experience and exposure will help you build your DJ service.

Mobile Beat magazine (800-836-9355) is a good resource for disc jockey services.

Driveway repair service

What will I be doing?

This type of service repairs driveways and other asphalt and concrete surfaces for homes and businesses. Fortunately, the driveway repair business doesn't require much equipment, yet it pays well. Unfortunately, this fact has drawn many con artists who slap asphalt down and demand hundreds of dollars for their minimal efforts.

What will I need to start?

Repairing asphalt and concrete driveways requires skill. To offer an honest driveway repair service, learn what you can about how roads and driveways are constructed, why they develop pot holes and fissures and what to do about them. Also research and select quality materials that can be easily applied and stand up to use.

Depending on the type of repairs you do, you may be able to carry needed materials in the trunk of your car. One driveway repair service owner built a plywood box that fit in the trunk to keep materials from damaging the car. He also built a canvas flap on one side of the box that would lay over the rear of the car, minimizing damage from spillage.

Who will my customers be?

Most of your customers will be individuals owning homes that require driveway repair services. You can spot them by driving through residential neighborhoods. As you do so, place a sign on the side of your car and include your local address, so prospects know you're not a con artist recently featured on *60 Minutes*.

One enterprising individual with a driveway repair service found that his community had recently been hit by a series of driveway repair cons. He convinced the local newspaper to do a story on how to avoid such cons and what to do to get legitimate repair. He canvassed his town with copies of the published article and marketed his services with a unique offer: Have the repair done now and don't pay for 30 days. By offering trust to customers, he was able to overcome their distrust of driveway repair services.

Other driveway repair services specialize in businesses, focusing on repairs and line-striping in parking lots.

How much should I charge?

The typical hourly rate for driveway repair services is $30 to $40. However, most services charge by the size of the job. One service has a fee for each of three pot hole sizes: fist, foot and two feet. "Two feet" means he can stand with both of his feet in the pothole. He doesn't quote this rate to the customer. He simply walks the driveway, adding up how many fist-size and foot-size pot holes need repair, then quoting a total price on the entire job.

How much will I make?

An established driveway repair service will require only 10 to 20 percent of the owner's time to sell repair jobs. The rest of the time will be billable. Overhead expenses will range from 25 to 50 percent, depending on what type of work is done and what tools are required. A repair service that needs a portable concrete mixer must charge more than a service that can rely on bags of ready-mix concrete. Typically, a Saturday every week can earn you a net profit of up to $10,000 a year.

How can I get started?

To start a driveway repair service, know your trade. You are selling your labor, but you are also selling your knowledge. If homeowners knew exactly how to make professional driveway repairs, many would do it themselves. The more you know, the more satisfied your customers will be—and the more money you will make.

If you have experience with asphalt or concrete, let your customers know of it. Help them overcome their natural reluctance to spend money by helping them understand the value of what you do and how they will benefit.

Floral service

What will I be doing?

There are nearly 50,000 floral services in the U.S. Most of them entered the business because they enjoy working with flowers and with people. How can you operate a home business in what is traditionally a retail storefront business? You can offer supporting services.

For example, your home-based floral business may arrange or deliver flowers for florist shops. Or you may grow them at your home and sell them wholesale to the shops or to floral wholesalers. Or you may produce products sold through florist shops, such as vases, dry-flower arrangements or trim products.

What will I need to start?

To successfully start a floral service you'll need to know your products, whatever they are. You may specialize in potted geraniums or in holiday arrangements. Whatever your specialty, you must know much more about it than your customers. The more you know, the more you will profit.

You will also need skills, resources and equipment. If you're a flower arranger, you'll need related skills, flowers to arrange and a work area. If you offer delivery services, you'll need to have a vehicle, a safe driving record and knowledge of the area, and you'll need to be available for quick deliveries.

Who will my customers be?

Customers for your floral service will include individuals (for weddings and funerals, for example), businesses, churches and other groups. Some home-based floral services specialize in a type of product or customer. One successful service owner provided floral arrangements for area churches on a contract basis. Each week featured a new arrangement. Because the arrangements for all her customers were the same, she was able to buy in quantity at the nearby floral wholesale market. She bought on Saturday morning, arranged all day Saturday and delivered early Sunday morning.

Determining the customers of your floral service will depend on what you sell.

How much should I charge?

Floral services typically establish an hourly rate of $25 to $60, but price by the arrangement. Others use multipliers, such as four times wholesale. Others, especially floral services that are starting out, price slightly lower than competitors in order to develop business.

For more specific information on pricing floral services, read my book, *Upstart Guide to Owning and Managing a Florist Service* (Upstart Publishing).

How much will I make?

Your florist service will require 10 to 30 percent of your time for marketing, depending on what you provide and to whom you sell. That means that 70 to 90 percent of the time you devote to your business is billable. You'll probably need more marketing time as you begin, but you may eventually spend less as your reputation grows.

Overhead costs vary greatly, depending on the type of product or service you provide. If you're producing arrangements on your kitchen table, overhead will probably be low. Including taxes, it may be as low as 20 percent. However, if you need a shop or delivery equipment, overhead may take 40 to 50 percent of every dollar you make. Even so, a part-time floral service can earn $10,000 or more in extra income each year. Some do even better.

How can I get started?

To start your business, first learn your trade. If you are selling your arrangement skills, attend a floral trade school or read up on these skills and get a job in the industry. Keep an eye out for opportunities in the industry where you would like to serve others—and make money from home.

The SIC code for floral services is 5992-01.

Food delivery service

What will I be doing?

This is a take-out society. Every year, the number of meals eaten away from home increases—as does the number of restaurant meals eaten at home. This is where a food delivery service can make money.

A food delivery service, obviously, delivers prepared foods to customers. Not as obvious is the related services a food delivery business can offer: grocery delivery, video delivery, even package delivery.

What will I need to start?

To deliver food to homes, you'll need not only a vehicle, but one that can carry food safely and efficiently. Because of fuel fumes, the food should not be placed in the trunk, but should ride with the driver. For a part-time venture, you can build a small insulated box that can be placed level on the passenger seat.

You may also need a food handler's license or certificate and maybe a commercial vehicle license, depending on your state and county requirements. Who would tell if you were using your car without proper licensing? Your competition!

You will also need a cellular telephone, so customers can contact you while you're on the road.

Who will my customers be?

Who will hire you to deliver food and other perishables? In most cases, you'll be working for the restaurants who want to sell more take-out food. Your customers may also include caterers and individuals.

One successful food delivery service specialized in delivering fast food products made and sold at a local shopping mall. The owner/driver picked up orders at the back door, placed them in insulated boxes and headed out. The restaurants knew that the service would be at the back door on the hour and half hour between 4 and 9 p.m. seven days a week, so they timed food preparation to match these times. Customers knew it, too, and called in orders asking for delivery.

In a smaller town with fewer restaurants, one enterprising delivery service owner took lunch orders for a factory, then placed the orders with area restaurants and timed delivery for noon. Another developed a pizza-and-a-movie order system that kept her busy on weekends.

How much should I charge?

You should establish an hourly rate of $20 to $40 for your food delivery service, but price in other ways. Some services charge the restaurant a percentage of the bill, typically about 20 percent, with a minimum delivery charge of $2 per delivery. Others charge by mileage, comparable to the price established by local taxi companies. A few specialize in one or two restaurants, contracting by the hour. Tips are kept by the driver.

How much will I make?

Hustle is the name of this business. If you can safely and efficiently deliver food when people want it, you can make good money—and it's even better with tips. In fact, part-time food delivery services can earn $12,000 to $15,000 a year for the owner after paying overhead expenses. Make sure that you drive within the speed limit and obey other traffic laws, however—especially if the name of your service or that of a restaurant is on the side of your vehicle.

How can I get started?

To start a food delivery service, begin studying local opportunities. Find out if someone else is already offering such a service and, if so, determine how you can do it better or for a different customer. Also consider cooperating with another delivery service, defining territories that are efficient for both while combining your marketing efforts.

Also look at unique ways to promote your service with a catchy name ("Dan's Mobile Diner") or symbol (a chef on a bicycle). The more people see your delivery vehicle—clean and safely driven—the more they will think of you when they want restaurant food at home.

Once you've designed and tested your food delivery service, produce a brochure or flier and hand it out to restaurants that may hire your business. Also have friends call restaurants and ask if they offer delivery service.

Freight broker

What will I be doing?

It's magic. Products made in far-off countries appear in retail stores even in the smallest communities. How do these products get from point A to point B? By ship, train and truck, of course. But there's another part of this process that many aren't aware of: those who make sure that the products are transported efficiently and economically. These are freight brokers.

There are nearly 10,000 freight brokers, consolidators and forwarding services in the U.S. They offer related services that require managing the contacts and the paperwork to move things from where they are to where they should be.

What will I need to start?

This isn't a business for everyone. It's best started by someone with experience in the transportation industry. One successful freight broker is a line-haul truck driver who wanted to get off the road. He now controls thousands of truckloads each year from his home office.

To start a freight brokerage, forwarding or consolidating service you'll need to know the industry and its players. Depending on your experience, you may decide to specialize in LTL (less than a truckload), containerized or shipload freight services. You can learn some things about this business in books, but practical experience and contacts in the industry are vital.

Who will my customers be?

Who will hire you for freight services? In most cases, it will be manufacturers or wholesalers who want to move products to market. An equipment manufacturer may need to move large equipment to a buyer. A wholesaler may need a shipment of socks moved from Taiwan to the distribution center in Cincinnati. A company may need its exhibit equipment moved to a trade show in Dallas and back.

Once identified, you can reach customers through mailing lists, ads in trade publications and through referrals.

How much should I charge?

The hourly rate for freight services has a broad range: $30 to $50 or more. In most cases, pricing of freight services is based on a percentage of the freight bill. These percentage fees vary as well, with higher percentages paid for smaller shipments. The fee also varies based on whether you are forwarding, consolidating or brokering freight. In most cases, the marketplace will dictate your fee. If your calculations say it is profitable, go for it.

How much will I make?

Once your freight business is established, less than 20 percent of your time will be spent marketing your services. As your business grows, you may need even less time as repeat and referral business builds. Because you don't buy the freight you're shipping, your overhead costs are low. A home office with a telephone, computer, supplies and taxes to pay will eat up 20 to 40 percent in overhead expenses.

How can I get started?

Again, this isn't everyone's home business. You will be paid in direct proportion to your knowledge of this industry and your ability to get things done. If your interest lies in freight brokering, learn your trade, develop organization and contact skills, work for someone else until you learn the business, then work for yourself.

The SIC codes are 4213-03 for freight brokers, 4731-02 for freight consolidators and 4731-04 for freight forwarders.

Fund raiser

What will I be doing?

If you want to be paid for helping many others, consider applying your people skills as a fund raiser.

Fund raisers help increase donations made to specific charities that are your clients. The fund raiser may consult with the charity, suggesting ideas that will encourage people to give. Or the fund raiser may actually do the collecting. Some fund raisers prefer one over the other and specialize.

What will I need to start?

To be a successful fund raiser you'll need people skills. You'll need to understand marketing and the special requirements and rules of raising funds. You'll need one or more telephones, mailing equipment or a mailing service, a plan for raising funds and, of course, someone to raise funds for.

Who will my customers be?

You will be raising funds for national or local nonprofit organizations. If national, you may become their local chapter. Contact organizations for which you'd like to raise funds and offer your services. Many larger organizations already have someone offering this service, but some don't. Many use unpaid volunteers managed by paid coordinators. State and local nonprofit organizations offer greater opportunities for your services.

How much should I charge?

Your hourly rate for fund raising will probably be $20 to $35, depending on your expenses. However, most fund raisers are paid a percentage of the funds they raise. Your percentage will probably be from 2 to 20 percent. Fund raising for individuals typically earns a higher percentage fee than for corporations.

Unfortunately, unscrupulous con artists purchase the right to raise funds for police benevolent associations and other groups, keeping as much as 80 percent of what they collect. This is not only dishonest, it makes your job more difficult because more people are distrustful of fund-raising contacts.

Help people overcome this initial distrust and you will be helping them contribute to worthwhile causes while you earn a fair return for your efforts.

How much will I make?

Once you've established clients, most of your time will be billable. Until then, expect to spend 25 to 50 percent of your time contacting and marketing your services to nonprofit organizations. Overhead will vary greatly, depending on who pays telephone and mailing expenses—you or the client. If you do, your percentage of funds raised should be higher because your costs are higher.

How can I get started?

The first step in fund raising is to determine if your state or city requires a license for fund raising. You may need to get certification from an organization that watches over charities. Contact your state business licensing agency for specific information.

To start your fund-raising service you'll first need a client. Consider any service or charitable organization you currently support or would like to support. Contact them to find out how you can serve them and what fees they are willing to pay. Then, based on your primary client's needs and your goals, establish a telephone or mailing campaign to raise funds and a system for tracking income.

The SIC code for fund-raising services is 8399-07.

Furniture refinishing

What will I be doing?

Making quality furniture is a craft that few master. If you enjoy working with fine furniture, but don't yet have all the skills to make it, consider a part-time furniture *refinishing* business. It will help you develop your ideas and skills as you pay your way.

There are nearly 9,000 full-time furniture refinishing services in the U.S. and many thousands more working part-time from their home or garage. A furniture refinishing service strips, repairs and refinishes furniture made by others. Some specialize in one aspect of refinishing, such as stripping, and leave the rest to other crafters. Some do it all, but focus on reselling what they refinish.

What will I need to start?

Refinishing furniture requires skills that can be self-taught with the help of books or some classes. It also requires supplies and equipment readily available: strippers, sanders and finishes. Many refinishers start out as hobbyists, buying old furniture at garage sales and turning it into "new" furniture for profit. In fact, some refinishers fund their business by doing this. They can then afford the sand blasters, dip tanks and spray booths required for larger refinishing jobs.

Who will my customers be?

Initially, you will probably refinish furniture for individuals. A small advertisement in a local newspaper can get you telephone calls. However, most refinishers also work with commercial accounts, refinishing furniture for antique stores and dealers. Some refinishers specialize in this market, depending on local market conditions.

Your customers may also include new furniture stores. One successful refinisher used Saturdays to make the rounds of all furniture stores in his area. He repaired furniture damaged in transit, touched up pieces damaged on the display floor and took referrals for repairs in customers' homes.

How much should I charge?

The hourly rate for furniture refinishing is $30 to $60, depending on the equipment required to do the job. A refinishing box with spray paints and touch-up sticks costs less to buy than a spray booth, so you should charge more when you use the booth.

Most jobs are estimated by the time it will probably take to complete, but are quoted as a set price. If you are doing standardized jobs, consider setting a standard price, such as $35 each for refinishing nightstands.

Once you've learn the trade, consider pricing by value. For example, refinishing a French vanity may take you only a few hours, but may add hundreds of dollars in value. If so, set your price as a portion of the added value.

How much will I make?

Furniture refinishing is a business that typically takes a while to develop, especially if competition is high in your area. You may spend 25 to 50 percent of your time during the first few months marketing your services. Once established, you may only spend 10 percent or less of your time trying to get new customers.

Overhead expenses for this business depend on the services you offer and the equipment needed. In most cases, overhead expenses, including taxes, will range from 20 to 40 percent of income—higher if you have an extensive shop.

A part-time furniture refinishing business can net you an income of $15,000 to $25,000 a year. If it gets to the higher end, consider turning your weekend business into a full-time one.

How can I get started?

The first step to starting a furniture refinishing business is to build your knowledge and skills. The second step is to start gathering your tools and supplies. If you have a successful technique for refinishing a specific type of furniture, use it to establish your business, then branch out once it is profitable.

Your work will usually advertise your skills. You should also place small service ads in local newspapers, but most of your better prospects will come from your better customers.

The SIC code for furniture refinishing is 7641-05.

Garage sale consultant

What will I be doing?

In many communities, garage sales are social events. For many people, they're certainly not financial events. Days of work are followed by a day of sitting and haggling. The income is small and unsold items are donated or discarded.

If your garage sales are successful, consider helping those whose sales aren't. Become a garage sale consultant. You won't get rich, but you can provide valuable services and make some money at a job you enjoy.

A garage sale consultant helps individuals plan, price and promote garage, estate and other sales. Some consultants will also sit at the garage sale for a percentage of sales income. Some handle the advertising as well, printing up weekly sheets of area garage sales and passing them out on Thursdays and Fridays.

What will I need to start?

A garage sale consulting business combines financial and social knowledge and skills. You must know how to price products, how to negotiate or teach others to negotiate, how to advertise and how to organize. If this describes you, consider starting a garage sale consulting business.

Who will my customers be?

Your customers will usually be people who want to turn unwanted household items into cash. Some do so to clear out the garage, while others put on sales to raise money. Advertise your services in local newspapers. Ask your customers to post your sign at their sales: "Another successful garage sale designed by..."

You may also work with a local radio station or newspaper, coordinating garage sale advertising and posting signs at each sale mentioning the media sponsor: "Listen to KXYZ radio Saturdays at 8 a.m. for this week's Garage Sale Show, hosted by..."

How much should I charge?

The hourly rate for garage sale consultants directly relates to the value provided to customers. The typical range is $25 to $40 an hour. Most events are priced by a commission on sales, ranging from 10 to 25 percent. The lower fee is for consulting and the higher includes advertising and promotion. You'll need a contract with your customers, drawn up in simple terms by an attorney, limiting your liability.

How much will I make?

The financial success of your garage sale consulting business is difficult to estimate, because there are so many variables. However, once established, your business should earn you $200 to $300 in net profits each weekend during the local garage sale season. You can extend your profits into other seasons by holding indoor flea markets and other sales, renting tables to crafters as well as those wanting to sell unused items.

How can I get started?

As with other part-time businesses, start your business by learning as much as you can about it. Visit area garage sales and look for opportunities. How would you advise each sale operator to make the event more profitable? Keep a notebook of ideas. Select a sign design that seems to work best. Find the most successful sales in your area and learn from their ads, signs, displays and pricing. Ask questions. Take notes. Read books on garage sales. Be an expert.

Also talk with local newspapers and radio stations about advertising rates and promotional opportunities. You may be able to get free or low-cost advertising for promoting them at your clients' garage sales.

Make sure, of course, that you're legal. Talk with city hall or county offices about necessary permits. If they're required, permit filings may be a great list from which to develop potential customers. You may also offer clients the service of filing for needed permits on their behalf.

Garden tiller

What will I be doing?

If you're a gardener, you know what's needed every year to prepare your vegetable or flower garden for planting. You've probably thought that it would be great if someone would do this work for you—except that you really do enjoy it. If this is so, consider offering your garden preparation services to others for a fee.

A garden tilling service prepares gardens for planting, turning the ground and adding nutrients as needed. You may return in the fall to clean up clients' gardens and prepare them for winter. You may also offer garden tending services, taking care of gardens while owners are away on vacation. There are many related services you can offer.

In larger communities, you may want to specialize in vegetable or flower gardens or in larger plots. You may simply till the soil or you may analyze gardens and feed them nutrients. Or you might specialize in setting up new gardens, clearing brush or weeds away so they don't soon return. What do you most enjoy doing in the garden? What are you willing to do for others in exchange for money?

What will I need to start?

To till and tend a garden you must know something about gardens. However, you don't have to be an expert gardener. If you have a tiller of your own or one to rent, you can simply offer that service. Once you've developed advanced gardening skills and experience, you can offer them to others.

Who will my customers be?

Your customers will be individuals who need gardens prepared for growing. Once established, you can contact old customers each year to get their business, as well as referrals. In the meantime, a small service advertisement in a local newspaper will help your services become known.

You may also contract your services to a group of condo owners or others who collectively garden a plot of ground. By tilling for many clients at the same location, you can reduce the fee paid by individual gardeners.

How much should I charge?

The hourly rate for garden tilling is usually $25 to $35. However, most tillers quote price by the area to be tilled. For example, a 12 x 20 foot plot that requires an hour to till can be priced at 15 cents a square foot or $36 for the job. Newer gardens may require a higher rate (because they take more time) and those that you prepare in the fall should get a lower rate (they take less time).

How much will I make?

Only 10 to 20 percent of your time will be needed to market your garden tilling service once the business is established. Your season will be short, so you will be quite busy for a few weeks a year. However, during that time, you should be able to net $5,000 to $10,000 if you're willing to work long evenings and weekends.

Study soils in your area and you may find that soil in one part of town is dry and ready for planting earlier than in another part of town. If so, plan your jobs accordingly. It will allow you to increase efficiency and reduce travel time between jobs.

How can I get started?

First, decide what services you will offer and how much you will charge. Then decide how best to promote your business. Some successful tillers offer tips on garden tilling to the local newspaper for inclusion in their spring garden issue. You will tell readers how best to prepare for planting and, of course, mention your services. Your ad near the article will tell readers how and when to contact you.

Make sure you have both a working tiller and working transportation for the tiller. A small tiller may fit in your car's trunk, but a larger one may require a truck or trailer to move.

Plan in the winter for your springtime business.

Giftwrapping service

What will I be doing?

Everybody loves getting gifts. But not everyone loves wrapping them. If you do, consider offering your talents to others with a home-based giftwrapping service.

A man injured in an industrial accident was confined to a wheelchair, limiting his employment opportunities. One thing he always enjoyed doing was wrapping presents, a job he gladly did for family and friends. One day, a friend asked if he would wrap presents for another family the friend knew. Yes, he would, for the cost of wrapping paper plus a few dollars. So began his wrapping business that spread by word-of-mouth advertising to the point that now he is frequently booked up for weeks before major holidays. His new hourly rate gives him a good part-time income.

What will I need to start?

Wrapping presents is a skill that can be learned. Larger colleges with adult education classes sometimes offer evening courses in gift-wrapping. There are also books and videos available on the topic that can be ordered through most bookstores.

Besides knowledge of wrapping designs and materials, you'll need to develop your skills through practice. Buy some leftover Christmas wrap and materials and a few gift boxes, then practice. Find a unique touch you can add that will identify your handiwork. You can also buy small stickers through stationery stores that say "Wrapped for you by...," but make sure it's okay with your customer to put the sticker on the box. Some would prefer to take credit for the nice wrapping job you've done.

Wrapping materials can be purchased through craft and gift shops until you can find a wholesale source for them.

Who will my customers be?

Your customers will depend on how and where you conduct your business. Some gift-wrappers require that individuals drop packages off at the house and pick them up the following day. Other gift-wrappers have small display booths that can be set up in malls during holiday seasons. Some will set up in major stores and be paid either by the stores or the customers.

Once you've decided who your customers will be, finding them should be easier. If customers need to come to you, advertise in the service section of local newspapers and make sure every customer gets a brochure and business card so they will refer others to you.

How much should I charge?

The hourly rate for efficient giftwrapping is typically $20 to $40. In most cases, wrappers establish prices by package size or value. Some experience with wrapping gifts will soon identify standard prices. One enterprising wrapper has boxes in four different sizes on the wall behind her booth with the prices clearly marked on each. As people step up, they ask for "#2 in birthday paper" or "#3 wrapped for a bridal shower," reducing the time needed to service each customer.

How much will I make?

How much you make depends on how much you wrap, when and where. A home wrapping service that requires customers to drop off gifts will earn less than one that sets up in a busy mall during the holiday seasons. Gross income can range from $1,000 to $10,000 or more for a small giftwrapping service, and even more once the business is built up. In fact, the wheelchair-bound wrapper mentioned earlier not only established a booth at a local mall, but also set up booths at other area malls and hired friends in wheelchairs to do the work. His income is more than $20,000 a year for seasonal work.

How can I get started?

Knowledge is power. Develop your knowledge of this craft through classes and practice. Find sources of materials. Study your competitors. Work as a wrapper in a store for one season. Then go to work for yourself. Advertise and promote what you do.

The SIC code for giftwrapping services is 7299-11.

Handyperson service

What will I be doing?

Some people love variety. They want a business that will challenge them every day. They enjoy being a jack- or jill-of-all-trades. If this describes you, consider being a handyperson. Many people need someone who is "handy" to do a variety of odd jobs for them: hauling, painting, fixing, building, stacking or trimming.

What will I need to start?

To be handy is to be skilled with your hands. To be a handyperson is to have a variety of skills and to be willing to learn new ones. The more you learn the more you earn.

To start a handyperson service you will also need some tools and transportation, such as a pickup truck. One enterprising handyperson took the back seat out of an old family sedan, removed the barrier between the seat and the trunk and was able to haul everything from plywood and lumber to cans of paint.

Gather your tools together. You may have all the tools you need right now. A handyperson who was asked to paint a shed purchased the equipment needed for the job and was able to use the equipment for dozens of later painting jobs.

You may also need a license or permit. Check with the state or local contractor licensing board to find out. Remember that licensing is intended to protect your customers. Make the best of it.

Who will my customers be?

As a handyperson, most of your customers will probably be homeowners. You may decide to specialize in helping homeowners in a specific part of your town. Or you may prefer cleaning and hauling jobs over painting and wallpapering. One handyperson may decide to work for shop owners as they renovate an older downtown commercial area. Another handyperson might do cleanup work on weekends at a small industrial park, taking loads of scrap to the dump or used boxes to the recycler.

If you decide who you prefer to work with, then finding them will be much easier. If your customers live in a certain geographic area, spend a weekend or two taking your flier door to door. Talk with potential customers and find out what types of jobs they need.

How much should I charge?

A handyperson can establish an hourly rate of $20 to $50, depending on skills and equipment. For example, a handyperson who tends lawns with little equipment requirements may be on the low side of the scale, while one with a hauling truck and lots of skills and tools may be on the higher side.

With experience, you'll find that you're doing the same three or four types of jobs over and over. This will help you become more efficient and make your estimates more accurate. You can then look at a job and quote an accurate price to the customer without revealing your hourly rate.

For example, you may say to a customer, "Trimming up these bushes will cost just $15 if I can do it next week when I'm in the neighborhood." You calculated the job as needing a half hour, with an hourly rate of $30. The customer calculates that the same job would take him two hours and is willing to trade the 15 bucks for two extra hours on the golf course. Everybody wins.

How much will I make?

Initially, you will spend most of your time finding customers and jobs. Once established, about 25 percent of your time will be needed for marketing your services and quoting jobs. Your overhead expenses will depend on the cost of your equipment and the amount of advertising you must do to attract business. Overhead expenses, including taxes, will range from a low of 20 percent to as much as 50 percent of every dollar of income.

Remember that the key to any successful business is managing expenses.

How can I get started?

First, decide whether you need licenses, permits or bonding for your handyperson service. If so, get them—or at least know how to get them once you're ready to start your business.

Second, identify your knowledge and skills. Then think about who might be willing to trade money for these skills. Talk to a few of these people. Ask them what they would be willing to pay for specific jobs. Estimate the time needed for each job and decide whether you can earn a fair fee for your time. If so, start your customer search.

Housecleaning service

What will I be doing?

There are many reasons why people need a housecleaning service. If you have the skills to efficiently clean houses—or are willing to learn them—you can set up a home-based housecleaning service for extra cash.

A housecleaning service cleans windows, washes floors and counters, vacuums carpets and dusts furniture and drapes. Some cleaning services specialize in homes, others do apartments and a few specialize in cleaning offices and other businesses.

There are nearly 28,000 full- and part-time housecleaning services in the U.S.

What will I need to start?

You may have all the basic cleaning equipment you need in your home right now. You may also have the needed supplies, but not in economical quantities. Shop the discount warehouse stores or whole-sale janitorial supply stores. The janitorial suppliers may even recommend supplies needed for certain tasks or offer techniques for using supplies more efficiently.

Make sure you have efficient cleaning skills. To earn the highest hourly rate, you will need to develop skills that help you get the jobs done quickly and thoroughly. Books like *Clutter's Last Stand* (Betterway Books) are helpful.

Who will my customers be?

Customers for your housecleaning service are homeowners and apartment renters. For efficiency, you may prefer to specialize in homes within a certain geographic area to limit time between jobs. Your customers may also be home buyers or renters referred to you by real estate agents in your area.

You can reach potential clients with fliers taken door-to-door and to local real estate offices. As you give a flier out, ask if there are any jobs you can bid on while you're there. You may get a job on the spot.

How much should I charge?

The typical hourly rate for housecleaning services is $25 to $45. The higher rate goes to experienced cleaners who have developed shortcuts and lots of referral business. Until then, establish your rate on the lower end of the scale, depending on the equipment you need for the jobs you do.

As with other home-based businesses, you probably won't quote your hourly rate to the customer. Instead, you will give a single price for the job. However, you will set that price by multiplying the estimated time (based on your experience) by your hourly rate.

"I can vacuum the entire house, dust furniture and drapes, clean floors and counters, wash all windows inside and out and clean bathrooms for just $95 per visit." You've calculated that you can do the jobs in three hours at $30 an hour and use about $5 in supplies. The customer is thinking all that work will take you an entire day. You're hired!

How much will I make?

Your housecleaning service will market itself in repeat and referral business once it is established. Allow about six months to get it going. Until then, plan on spending up to half of your time promoting your business and bidding on jobs.

Your overhead expenses will range from 25 to 50 percent of gross income, depending on the cost of your equipment and supplies. Taxes are included as well, although they vary depending on where you live.

How can I get started?

Start your housecleaning service by getting yourself organized for efficient cleaning. Gather the tools and materials you will need and learn how to use them efficiently.

Next, produce fliers that tell what you do, how much you charge and how to contact you. Circulate them to potential customers.

Always be looking for ways to promote your business. Take your fliers to area home shows. Offer cleaning services to offices and small businesses. Give your brochures to friends and neighbors. Talk to someone at your local newspaper, giving them tips on cleaning that they can pass on to readers.

The SIC code for house- and office-cleaning services is 7349-02.

House-painting service

What will I be doing?

Painting is one of the jobs that most people don't like to do. It's messy, it takes time, it's boring and it means working on a ladder.

If painting is fun for you—or at least not a chore—consider offering a house-painting service.

A house-painting service paints residential interiors and/or exteriors. It may also paint commercial buildings. It has the equipment, skills and experience to do a good job at a fair price.

What will I need to start?

To start a house-painting service you must have experience in the trade. Maybe you've been a painter for someone else and now want to work for yourself. Or maybe you've painted so many of your own homes or apartments that your experience level is high. Even so, read more and practice more. You won't be paid as much for your painting skills as for your painting efficiency.

You'll need some equipment: brushes and rollers, sprayer, etc. You'll also need work clothing. In addition, you will need paints and maskings, but those can be purchased as you do the jobs.

Who will my customers be?

It's pretty easy to spot potential customers for an exterior painting service. One successful painter simply drove through neighborhoods in the springtime, looking for houses that showed signs of needing painting. He then gave quotes to the owners and suggested that they schedule jobs by June 1 to ensure completion over the summer. In the fall he followed up with his exterior customers to find out if they needed interior painting over the winter months.

A small service ad in the local newspaper and your business card on area bulletin boards can help potential customers identify themselves.

How much should I charge?

House painters get paid well. This is because of the skills and equipment they need, as well as the fact that most people don't want to do the job themselves.

The hourly rate for a house-painting service is $35 to $75. Most jobs are quoted by size or complexity, once you estimate the time needed. Learn from each job, calculating what you should have charged and how to price more accurately in the future. Some painters calculate the square footing on the main floor then multiply it by their pricing factor. If there is a second floor or dormers, the surface area to be painted is multiplied by a factor of 1.5 or 2, depending on how difficult it will be to paint.

A smart painter drove around until he found a painting job in process, then interviewed the owner about pricing. A few calculations netted not only a fair pricing factor, but also guided him in setting his own hourly rate.

How much will I make?

Marketing your services will take much of your effort until you get a few jobs. Then you will probably be able to keep busy by spending 10 to 20 percent of your time looking for new jobs. If your pricing is reasonable and your work is good, referral business will be your marketing.

Overhead costs will range from 25 to 40 percent, depending on equipment and whether you include the cost of paint in your bid. Some quote a labor charge, with paint and supplies extra.

How can I get started?

You must be more than just a painter to succeed at this business. You must be an *efficient* painter. Develop your skills. Learn techniques that reduce time without reducing quality. Learn from each job you do. Buy quality equipment that will save you time in the long run.

Let others know that you're in business to paint houses. Many customers will come to you.

Read *Painting Contractor: Start and Run a Money-Making Business* by Dan Ramsey and Walter Curtis (TAB/McGraw-Hill).

The SIC code for house-painting services is 1721-01.

House-sitting service

What will I be doing?

A house-sitting service watches vacant homes to minimize burglary or damage. Depending on the client's needs, you may simply drive by slowly once a day and pick up mail and newspapers or actually stay in the home while the owners are gone. Beyond the basic service, you can offer to feed and care for pets, water plants, check and forward telephone messages and important mail and even clean the house.

What will I need to start?

House-sitting requires few skills, but it does require honesty and trust. You may be required to be bonded and insured, depending on your clientele. Building a reputation as a trustworthy house sitter will build your business faster than paid advertising.

Some house sitters build a notebook of information useful to them in their business. They include the names of customers and potential customers, emergency contacts for each, the telephone numbers for emergency services and the location of hidden keys and codes for security systems. Protect this valuable book. You may also want a house-sitting kit that includes flashlights, household tools, notepads and pens and other resources that may come in handy as you check out a home.

Who will my customers be?

In most cases, your customers will be homeowners and apartment renters who will be leaving for more than a couple of days. Areas with more expensive homes may be good places to start working.

Some house sitters specialize in vacant homes that are currently for sale or lease through local real estate companies. Contact agencies in your area to discuss their needs. Don't forget to contact bankers who may have repossessed homes that are vacant and in need of watching.

How much should I charge?

The hourly rate for house-sitting is higher than you might imagine: $20 to $30. This is because watching a house really doesn't require much time. *In fact, watching six nearby homes may take you* less than an hour a day. If you are providing additional services (pet care, plant watering, lawn trimming, etc.), calculate your price based on your hourly rate. A weekly package that requires a total of two hours of your time can be fairly priced at $40 to $60 per week.

How much will I make?

You won't have to spend much time selling your services once you're established—typically 10 to 20 percent of marketing time. Expenses are very low, with overhead costs ranging from 10 to 20 percent. Most important, work efficiently, plan your services and offer value.

How can I get started?

There are probably many customers for your service already nearby. Once you've decided you want to build a house-sitting service, develop your product and your pricing, produce a flier telling others about it and get it into circulation.

A smart house sitter took her first flier to the local police department and asked to post it. If people calling in to notify police about going away on vacation asked, they were told about the house-sitting service and given a telephone number. The sitter benefited. The police benefited by the help. And most important, the house or apartment dweller benefited.

Importer

What will I be doing?

Thousands of people around the world come to America each year looking for the land of opportunity. Many unknowingly bring a great opportunity with them: business contacts in their native country. These contacts can often be used to build a business importing to the U.S.

A Russian engineer found a job in the U.S. with an industrial control manufacturer. He learned that his employer didn't have a reliable source for a component in pressure instruments. A few calls back to "the old country" brought samples, and he was soon importing components part-time.

What does an importer do? An importer helps overseas businesses and domestic buyers trade. There are more than 11,000 full- and part-time importers in the U.S.

What will I need to start?

To start an import business you must first have an idea of what you want to import. Look at products around you that you are most familiar with. Many are already imported. Others could be. Some importers specialize in trinkets for the flea market crowd, but many others find sources for products used in business and industry. Millions of dollars have been made by importers of computer components.

To learn the trade, begin reading books like *Starting an Import/Export Business* (Wiley). It includes a comprehensive glossary and list of resources on importing.

As an importer, you probably won't buy any products. You'll just help others buy them. So you typically won't need warehouse space or special equipment. But you will need a small home office, telephone and fax equipment and probably a computer and printer.

Who will my customers be?

Customers for your imported products will be manufacturers, retailers, consumers, mail order companies and other businesses, depending on what you're importing. Once you've decided what you'll be importing, identifying and finding customers will be much easier. For example, if you've found a unique gift item, contact mail order companies or start your own. If you've found a source for low-cost high-speed computer modems, offer them to a manufacturer or to computer shops that build their own computers.

How much should I charge?

This is a tough question. In most cases, you'll be paid a commission on the value of what you import for others. The commission can range from 3 to 12 percent or more. You can potentially make more money—or less—by importing goods and selling them yourself. Once established, your import business should give you a gross income of $30 to $50 an hour before overhead expenses.

How much will I make?

Because of the low overhead costs, importers typically make good money for their efforts—if they work smart. A part-time home-based importer can build a business to net $15,000 to $30,000 a year. Deduct office expenses and taxes of 20 to 40 percent.

How can I get started?

To start your import business, contact a U.S. Department of Commerce office near you, found in the government listings of metropolitan telephone books. You can also contact your regional Small Business Administration office for requirements and maybe some leads.

Build your business on paper before you build it in fact. Calculate, recalculate, research, interview, ask others and learn. You will be paid by what you know as much as what you do.

Finally, start contacting potential customers of your service, looking for opportunities to import products they need.

The SIC code for importers is 5099-05.

Income tax preparation service

What will I be doing?

There are more than 60,000 income tax preparation services in the U.S., many with offices, but many others doing tax work from their homes.

What does an income tax preparation service do? It gathers and prepares income tax information and advises clients on how to legally pay the least amount of taxes. All tax services handle federal income taxes and, if required, state income taxes. They help businesses calculate quarterly estimated tax payments. They make recommendations on reducing tax obligations.

What will I need to start?

To advise clients and prepare tax returns, you must understand the IRS tax codes. There are community college and adult education classes on income tax preparation available in most areas. Correspondence courses are also available. Because the code is so complex, most tax preparers specialize in one or two areas of it. Some help individuals prepare the annual *Form 1040*. Others specialize in helping small businesses with the *Schedule C* part of the *1040*. Others work with investors who have tax preparation questions.

To be an income tax preparer, you'll need knowledge, skills, resources (tax code books and aids), and equipment (a calculator, for example). You'll also need patience. There's no one more stressed than a tax payer, nor one so confident as a tax collector. You are the peace keeper.

Who will my customers be?

Your customers will be individuals, small businesses, organizations and groups. You'll find them by advertising your services and making it easy for them to find you. Most individuals start thinking about taxes in February, when the last of their *W-2s* arrive in the mail. Small businesses think of taxes mostly in December and January, but they also have to think about them quarterly. Large businesses think about them every day.

How much should I charge?

The hourly rate for income tax preparation services varies with the level of knowledge and skill offered. The typical range is $30 to $60 an hour. However, standardized tasks can be priced by the task. For example, preparing *1040s* for a married couple filing jointly with less than $100,000 in income and standardized deductions may typically take you three hours to prepare and file. If so, at an hourly rate of $40, you could price this service at $120.

To help you in pricing, find out what other income tax preparers in your area are getting for their services.

How much will I make?

Most people don't need to be sold on their need for income tax preparation services. They either need it or not. If so, basic advertising will bring customers to you at tax time—although you may want to advertise more the rest of the year to bring in more income. The point is that advertising costs won't eat up much of your income.

However, tools such as books and a computer will. Your overhead expenses will range from 20 to 45 percent, depending on who your customers are and whether you have the latest in computer systems.

How can I get started?

If you don't have training or experience in income tax preparation, take some classes and read some books. Read lots of books. As with other businesses, you will be paid by what you know.

Contact the National Association of Tax Practitioners (414-749-1040) for more information.

The SIC code for income tax preparation services is 7921-01.

Information broker

What will I be doing?

In today's economy, information is one of the most valuable commodities. Accurate information can help people make money on the stock market or in real estate and can enhance nearly any business.

Do you love to gather information? Are you a researcher by heart? If so, consider a home business as an information broker. Information brokers find and furnish valuable, hard-to-find information for specific customers.

What will I need to start?

To start an information brokerage service in your home, you'll first need to know how to find valuable information. Most information brokers use computers to search electronic databases, so you will probably need access to a computer and an understanding of how to use it. Some researchers start their business venture using public resources such as libraries, and may even use the computers at larger libraries.

Depending on the type of research you will be doing, you may need membership with online database services.

Who will my customers be?

Most information brokers specialize in one or more fields. If your background is in rocket science, you'll know how to find answers to specific questions about propulsion systems. If you have business experience, consider offering valuable information to businesses.

As an example, the owner of a successful pizza parlor was considering franchising her operation. An information broker helped her analyze other pizza franchises, discover the best location for a second store and identify attorneys who could help her with the legal aspects of franchising.

How much should I charge?

The hourly rate for information brokers is $40 to $100. Although a few charge less, there are many who charge more. The difference is the value of the information to your customer. If your customer has a curiosity about Continental Mark II automobiles, for example, he or she probably won't pay much for the information. But if a business needs information that will help them launch a new $1 million product line, your services will be very valuable.

Some information brokers charge by the hour, but others price by the project (based on estimated time) or by a percentage of the value of the information. To do so, a business information broker may ask a client what the resulting information will be worth to the buyer, then price it accordingly.

How much will I make?

Because many people don't even know how an information broker can help them, you will spend extra time educating prospects. In fact, 20 to 30 percent of your time will be needed for marketing and even more as you start up your business. Overhead expenses range from 20 to 50 percent, depending on whether you include research costs (online charges, books, photocopies) in your hourly rate or add them separately to the bill. Some customers want itemized expenses, while others prefer a single price. Remember, though, that if you tell your customers the source of your information they may decide to go directly to it next time.

A part-time information broker can net $10,000 to $30,000 a year working evenings and weekends. In fact, many online databases used by businesses are less expensive to access outside of normal business hours. These databases cost $20 to $150 an hour during the business day.

How can I get started?

Start learning how to research. Decide whether you will research online or the old-fashioned way. Decide who your customers will be and what they will want to know. Then find out where you can get the information for them with the least effort and expense. Finally, start contacting prospective customers to let them know about your services.

If you're uncomfortable with charging high hourly rates, offer discounted rates for the first few months of your business. By then your skills will be developed and your customers will see the value of your service. If you do offer a discount, trade it for a letter of recommendation.

Contact the Association of Independent Information Professionals (212-779-1855) for more information.

Interior-decorating service

What will I be doing?

If you have the skills or an interest in interior decorating, you can probably operate a decorating service from your home. With just a few hours a week, you can design and decorate homes, offices, retail stores or other places where people live and work. And you can be paid well for doing what you enjoy.

There are nearly 30,000 full-time interior-decorating services in the U.S., so there's lots of competition. But a well-respected decorator who offers service and value to a defined group of customers has no competition.

What will I need to start?

Of course, to start an interior-decorating service you must have both knowledge and experience in the field. That's what you're selling. The more you know, the more you can help—and the more you can make. So learn your trade with courses, books and practical experience as a decorator working for someone else. Learn what works and, just as important, what doesn't work.

Who will my customers be?

Your customers for interior-decorating services will be individuals, furniture stores, retail businesses, business offices and even churches. Decorators who try to do them all typically do few of them well. Specialize in serving the decorating needs of a specific group of customers where your skills and interests are strongest.

Once you've defined who your customers are, finding them is much easier. For example, if you prefer to decorate the homes of the rich and famous, start contacting the rich and famous in your area. If there aren't many, you may have to move to where there are, or you may need to expand to serve those who want others to *think* they're rich and famous.

How much should I charge?

Your hourly rate for an interior-decorating service will be $35 to $75. Most decorators stay on the lower end of this range for many years until they have too much business, then they increase rates until the amount of work is just about right.

Interior-decorating services often help customers establish a budget, then price services as a percentage of the budget. For example, an office complex that will spend $20,000 on redecorating may get a bill of 10 percent or $2,000 from the decorator. Other decorators charge the customer less, but get suppliers to sell to them at a discount.

Find out what your competitors are charging and price accordingly.

How much will I make?

You'll spend 20 to 30 percent of your time seeking new business. That leaves 70 to 80 percent of your time billable—once your business is off the ground. If you are only advising customers, not buying any of the merchandise yourself, your overhead costs (including taxes) will range between 20 to 40 percent. Advertising will take up more of your budget for the first year or two, then taper off as your name becomes better known.

How can I get started?

Pick a good business name, get your business licenses and permits, design a quality brochure and start promoting yourself in local news media. Be sure to join trade associations that give you credentials in your areas of specialization. Find a way of showing why your services are better than that of your competitors. If your customers are vanity buyers, make sure you get letters of recommendation from any of your customers who are well-known and respected in your community. If you're dedicated to quality service, you'll soon have a profitable business doing what you love.

The SIC code for interior-decorating services is 7389-02.

Inventory service

What will I be doing?

Computerized cash registers in stores not only add up the total cost of customer's purchases, they keep track of everything that has been sold. These computers manage a store's inventory and tell the owner what needs to be ordered.

However, most stores still need to take what is called a "physical inventory" every few months to a year. This inventory is done by people who walk through the store, physically counting the number of each item on the shelves. If you have some experience doing this work, consider operating an inventory service from your home.

There are about a thousand full-time inventory services in the U.S. Some hire independent contractors, rather than employees. You can operate your business as an independent contractor or by managing others to do the work.

What will I need to start?

Few skills are required for taking physical inventory. You must be accurate, conscientious and careful. You can gain experience by offering your services to local retailers willing to train you.

Depending on the type of inventory you manage, you may need handheld computers or bar code scanners to count and keep track of items by product number. Sometimes the warehouse or retailer will provide these tools. In other cases, you may be able to earn a higher income if you supply your own.

Who will my customers be?

Your customers will be retail and wholesale businesses with inventory. Because businesses have different operating or fiscal years, the work may be year-round with high and low points. Your customers will determine when and why they need a physical inventory taken.

Some inventory services travel. One successful service is operated by a couple from a motor home. Clients are contracted a few months in advance. The couple arrives at the site, takes physical inventory, enjoys some time off in a new town, then moves on to the next contracted job.

How much should I charge?

Inventory services have an hourly rate of $25 to $45, depending on what tools they provide and their efficiency at doing the job. Most price their service by the value of inventory or by a flat per-day fee.

How much will I make?

Finding customers will take 10 to 20 percent of your time, leaving 80 to 90 percent billable. Overhead expenses range from 10 to 35 percent, depending on what you provide and whether you must travel to the inventory site.

How can I get started?

The best way to learn this business is to do it as an employee. Look for inventory jobs in local newspapers. Ask friends who own businesses all you can about the inventory process and whether they take a physical inventory of stock.

Finally, develop fliers about your inventory service, including prices and experience, and circulate them to those who may need your services in the future. As you pass them out, ask businesses when they typically take physical inventory, then contact them about a month before that date. You may find yourself with new customers.

The SIC code for inventory services is 7389-62.

Janitorial service

What will I be doing?

The first janitors were door- or security-keepers in castles. As locks became more reliable, the castle owners must have said, "Grab a broom!" and the first modern janitors went to work.

Today, there are about 28,000 full-time janitorial services in the U.S., and many thousands more that operate part-time from homes across the nation. Most janitors serve the cleaning needs of businesses and stores, removing dust and dirt. This is an especially important job in today's work environment where dirt particles can damage sensitive computers and other electronic equipment.

The growing need for janitors has been matched by people who enjoy cleaning up. They get satisfaction from cleaning, straightening and recycling. If you are one of these neatniks, consider starting a home-based janitorial service.

What will I need to start?

The skills required for cleaning are few. However, to clean efficiently requires training and experience. You can develop on-the-job experience by working as a janitor for a school or office, or as an employee of a successful janitorial service.

The equipment needed depends on what type of janitorial service you offer. Many janitorial services specialize in stores, offices, industrial buildings, warehouses, schools, hospitals or other sites. Some services specialize in a type of cleaning, such as floors, carpets, walls and ceilings or glass. Defining what you do will help you determine what you need to start.

Fortunately, you can find much of the equipment and supplies you need at a single location: a wholesale janitorial supply store. In most cases, the supply store is operated by experienced janitorial service owners who can help you select equipment and supplies that are most efficient for what you do. Check area telephone books for janitorial suppliers.

Who will my customers be?

Your customers will be companies, individuals, municipalities, manufacturers, schools, hospitals and others. One small janitorial service lost a major contract and needed to replace the income to pay for floor-cleaning equipment just purchased. She decided to put the equipment to better use by specializing in stripping and waxing floors with a special polymer finish that offered both shine and durability. Within a couple of months, she had replaced the income from the large account with numerous smaller accounts that gave her business more stability.

If you are thinking about starting a general janitorial service for a specific retail area, talk to potential customers about their needs, their cleaning schedules, how much they pay for janitorial services and what it would take to earn their business. You may soon have your first customers lined up.

Some janitorial supply stores also work as job brokers, finding janitorial contracts and selling them to their customers. Ask supply stores if they also broker janitorial contracts.

How much should I charge?

The hourly rate for janitorial services is $25 to $60. However, most services quote prices based on the size of the job, frequency and skills needed. Square footage is a common measurement. However, the square-foot price for floor care is quite different from that for emptying trash cans. Consider taking on a few jobs for a low hourly rate until you develop the skills and experience to work efficiently and know how best to price jobs.

How much will I make?

Once you've developed contract jobs, most of your time will be billable. Until then, plan to spend as much as 30 percent of your time marketing your janitorial service. Overhead expenses typically range from 20 to 40 percent, depending on the equipment required.

How can I get started?

The difference between a profitable janitorial service and one that is nearly bankrupt is typically knowledge. Learn your trade, develop skills, learn to work efficiently, find out what your customers want. The more you know about your business and your customers, the more you will succeed with a janitorial service.

The SIC code for janitorial services is 7349-02.

Kitchen utensil-sharpening service

What will I be doing?

Nearly every kitchen in America has dozens of blades that are becoming dull and unsafe. A kitchen utensil-sharpening service can bring new life to old utensils and save the owners money.

This is a valuable business that is sometimes overlooked in a world of disposable products. A kitchen utensil-sharpening service sharpens and repairs knives, scissors, small appliance blades and other edges to make them as good as new at a fraction of the cost of replacement.

What will I need to start?

There are many good books and courses on sharpening available through local bookstores, libraries and correspondence schools. But nothing is more valuable than practical experience. A man who found a sharpening wheel and motor at a garage sale went to other sales looking for knives and kitchen utensils to sharpen. During the following week he taught himself to sharpen utensils with the wheel. The following weekend, he held his own garage sale offering cleaned and sharpened utensils and made a profit of more than $150. He spent the profits on advertising and soon built a small business in his garage sharpening utensils for others.

Watch local classified ads for used sharpening equipment for sale.

Who will my customers be?

Most of your customers will be people with kitchens full of un-sharpened utensils. They can be found by going house-to-house in your neighborhood offering to sharpen one utensil for free. When you bring the sharpened utensil back, most people will ask you to sharpen more.

You can also offer your services to resale stores, picking up used or donated utensils for sharpening and returning them in a few days. Use the same free-sample technique, then give the stores a per-piece price.

Once you've learned the techniques of sharpening, offer your services to restaurants in your area, sharpening their knives and other utensils. Knives are professional tools for chefs and they want them to be sharp to ensure efficiency.

How much should I charge?

You will charge for your sharpening services by the utensil, but you will estimate the price based on your hourly rate. The typical hourly rate for kitchen utensil-sharpening is $25 to $45, depending on skills and equipment. If you can sharpen a set of six kitchen knives in an hour at a rate of $30 an hour, you could price the job at $5 a knife.

How much will I make?

You won't get rich with a part-time kitchen utensil-sharpening service. You knew that. However, you can earn a good supplemental income and work your own hours. A service that sharpens six hours a week can bring the owner extra income of $5,000 to $10,000 a year. Tools are minimal and overhead expenses, once tools are purchased, are low.

How can I get started?

Find a book or a course on sharpening. Get a blade sharpener, ei-ther manual or motor-driven. Then grab all the utensils in your kitchen and start developing your skills. If you get a chance, learn from an experienced sharpener. One person learned sharpening from the owner of a local saw-sharpening service who wanted someone to take over knives and other utensils.

An ad in local service directories is typically all that's needed to let people know what you do. But don't expect them to rush to your door, because it will take many times seeing your ad before most people will consider calling you. Build word-of-mouth advertising as well.

The SIC code for sharpening services is 7699-28.

Lawn care service

What will I be doing?

Many homeowners consider their lawns an expression of themselves. They don't want weeds. They want nicely trimmed and greened lawns that reflect quality and care. You can help these fastidious people—and make some money in your spare time.

A lawn care service maintains and repairs lawns. Some services also trim shrubs and trees. If you enjoy yard work and lawn care, consider this part-time opportunity as a weekend money-maker. As important, see it as a chance to meet and help people while you work in the out-of-doors. There are at least 25,000 full-time lawn care services in the U.S. and probably twice that many operated part-time.

What will I need to start?

The skills required for basic lawn care are easily learned. What is important is to learn to work efficiently. Trimming a lawn well in half the time it normally takes will effectively double your per-hour income.

To cut lawns, you must first understand them. Learn as much as you can about grass seed, fertilizers, watering requirements, cutting lengths and related topics.

Make sure you have efficient equipment. A lawn service may have two lawn mowers, an edger, a spreader, hoses, sprayers and nozzles. Your investment will be $500 to $1,000, plus the cost of a vehicle to move equipment. The least expensive transportation is probably a small open trailer hitched to your car. If you work in a rainy area, consider a closed trailer that allows you to mount rakes and other equipment on the inside walls.

Who will my customers be?

Your customers will probably be homeowners, apartment managers, contractors, retail businesses, manufacturers' offices, schools and government offices.

One successful lawn care service volunteered to maintain a plot of land in the center of a small town, across from the courthouse. In exchange, the business posted a sign in the park noting who was voluntarily maintaining it. A story in the local newspaper followed. Not only was the park a clear example of the service's credentials, the sign was an excellent advertisement located in the center of town where everyone saw it.

How much should I charge?

Hourly rates for lawn care services range from $25 to $60. However, most services bid jobs by the size of the lawn and the amount and frequency of care. Trimming an 800-square-foot lawn may take 40 minutes at $30 an hour, so the service charges $20 (two-thirds of $30) or 2.5 cents a square foot. Additional services such as monthly feeding, weekly watering and thatching are also charged by the square foot, but calculated based on the service's hourly rate.

How much will I make?

A part-time lawn care service works with repeat and referral customers, minimizing marketing time. In fact, once established, a successful lawn care service may require only 10 percent of the owner's time to keep the business busy. The rest of the time is billable.

Overhead expenses will typically range from 15 to 35 percent, depending on the cost of equipment. One service started with a borrowed lawn mower and some hand tools, and required only gasoline. Once the business was established, new equipment was purchased and the hourly rated was adjusted accordingly.

How can I get started?

Start your lawn care service by going door-to-door offering your skills, then using the money you earn to purchase lawn care equipment. With every contact you make, you have a chance to build your client list and grow your company.

The SIC code for lawn care services is 0782-06.

Letter-writing service

What will I be doing?

Some people would rather face the dentist without Novocain than write a letter. If you actually enjoy writing letters—and others enjoy receiving them from you—consider offering your services as a letter writer.

A letter-writing service confidentially assists clients in communicating their thoughts and emotions. You will be helping people express their love, concern, criticism, knowledge, wisdom or gossip by the written word. You may do little more than revise someone's notes for clarity, spelling and grammar. Or you may help someone write to a congressional representative on a topic important to your customer.

What will I need to start?

Writing letters for others means you must know how to write well and you must know how to help people organize their thoughts. You may need to take a brush-up class in grammar or writing fundamentals.

What writing format you use (cursive or computer) depends on what you're most comfortable with and what your customers prefer. Some people cannot compose personal letters using something as mechanical as a keyboard. Others cannot do otherwise. So you'll need your chosen tools.

Who will my customers be?

It is surprising how many people today are functionally illiterate. That certainly doesn't mean that they are dumb. They may be quite articulate expressing their thoughts in their own spoken words, but they may have difficulty placing them on paper. Others simply need someone to help them focus thoughts and ideas.

One letter-writing service contracts with local upscale nursing homes to help patients write letters to relatives.

How much should I charge?

Your skills as a professional letter writer can earn an hourly rate of $20 to $35. You will price your services by the page, by the typical letter or by the purpose of correspondence. Most charge by the page or word. Rates range from 5 cents to 25 cents a word. A handwritten page of 100 words is charged at $5 and, if you can write five an hour, equals to about $25 an hour. A page written on a computer may include 250 words. At 5 cents a word, that's $12.50 a page and about a half hour of your time.

How much will I make?

Overhead expenses are minimal for a letter-writing service, unless you require a computer. In fact, a cursive service can keep expenses down to just 10 to 20 percent. Add a computer to the equation and expenses double, depending on how much work you get.

Even so, a part-time letter writer can quickly build the business to gross $6,000 to $10,000 a year, once the word gets out about your writing skills.

How can I get started?

To help others write their thoughts, you must know how the writing process works. You must also understand the type of correspondence you're doing. The process of writing a letter to your client's old friend is different than writing to a legislator. Fortunately, there are many good books on how to write effectively.

Of course, practice is important. Use your skills to write letters for yourself. In fact, select the best of these letters to show potential customers. If especially good, there are often elements of your letters that can be adapted to the needs of your customers.

How can people find out about your service? The best way is to write your own flier and circulate it to businesses, nursing homes, hospitals, institutions, schools and other places where people may need help writing letters.

Mail-order sales

What will I be doing?

Mail order isn't really a business. It's a *way* of doing business. It uses the mail service or package delivery services to market and distribute products. Unlike many unscrupulous businesses, the *legitimate* mail order business sells things people need and want by mail.

What will I need to start?

To sell by mail, you need a product or service that others want and are willing to buy and receive by mail. It must be a product or service that can be easily delivered. Elephants-by-Mail is a poor business idea. Elephant-Books-by-Mail is better.

You will need knowledge of shipping methods and costs. Some products are easier to ship than others. Some must be shipped economically, while others need to get to the customer fast. What shipping services you use depends on your customers' needs and willingness to pay.

Your mail-order business depends on your knowledge of marketing: how to find and keep customers. The more you know about reaching your customers, the less you will waste on unneeded advertising.

Who will my customers be?

Who will buy from you sight unseen? Those who have developed trust in you and who need a product they can't find otherwise. You may be the exclusive manufacturer of a product for fishermen. You may offer 100 percent satisfaction guaranteed on everything you sell. You may offer free overnight delivery. You may only sell to the affluent.

A Texas tamale maker dramatically expanded business by offering tamales by mail. I'm not kidding. The tamales, individually wrapped and frozen, are shipped via overnight freight to customers around the world. A brochure sells the product and a toll-free telephone number is used for ordering by credit card. FedEx does the rest. Sure, you can buy tamales at the local supermarket, but not *their* tamales.

How much should I charge?

It depends. In many cases, mail-order services have an hourly rate of $30 to $75. Most, however, prefer to use a markup or multiplier to cover the extra expenses of advertising and shipping. A common multiplier is three. That is, a product that wholesales for $10 is sold by mail for $30—or $29.95. Some mail-order businesses use lower or higher multipliers, but this one is the most popular.

How much will I make?

Mail-order businesses typically have a forgotten advantage over retail stores: S&H or shipping and handling. The mail-order price is $29.95 plus $4.95 shipping and handling. So the price is really $34.90, right? But most consumers probably compare apples and apples: $29.95. The point here is that you will often make more with mail-order products, because the customer is directly paying one of your major expenses—shipping and handling.

An efficient mail-order service can bring the owner an extra $5,000 to $25,000 a year in net income, depending on what is offered and how efficiently it is sold.

How can I get started?

My book, *Upstart Guide to Owning and Managing a Mail-Order Business* (Dearborn), includes hundreds of mail-order business ideas, as well as more specific information on pricing and marketing.

Masonry service

What will I be doing?

Concrete and brick are all around us. The people who install these products are called masons or masonry contractors. There are more than 11,000 masonry contractors in the U.S., many of whom started or now work on a part-time basis.

Masonry services design, install and maintain concrete, brick, rock and other masonry products. These products are included in buildings, fences, walls, sidewalks and other structures. If you have proven your masonry skills working for someone else, maybe it's time to consider working for yourself.

What will I need to start?

Masons need extensive skill and training for many jobs. However, other jobs, such as installing a brick or concrete walkway, can be done by the novice. You will only be able to sell the skills you have, so the first step to starting a masonry service is measuring your current skills and experience.

The second step is to gather tools and equipment you'll need. If you're repairing sidewalks, for example, you'll need a concrete mixer and concrete hand tools. If you're building block walls, you'll need mortar equipment and tools.

Who will my customers be?

As a mason employed by a company, you probably didn't have to worry about who your customers were. Your customer was your foreman.

You did what the foreman said, and everybody was happy. But when you market your masonry skills on your own, you must first determine who to sell to.

Customers for your masonry service depend on what services you offer. In most cases, your customers will be general contractors, remodeling contractors, homeowners, apartment owners, retail businesses, office building owners and manufacturing plants. Fortunately, once identified they can be contacted through listings in local telephone books or through regional contractor associations.

How much should I charge?

The rate for a masonry service varies greatly by skills, but typically ranges from $35 to $75 an hour. Subcontracted work is typically priced by the hour. However, many jobs are bid by the size of the job and the complexity of the product. A masonry wall might be priced by the block or by the surface. A concrete walk would be priced by the square foot and the thickness in inches. Some trades have locally standardized pricing with little variation, while others are more competitive.

How much will I make?

You'll find that 20 to 30 percent of your time will be spent looking for jobs. The figures may become less once you're well-established and you get repeat and referral business. However, they may be even higher when you begin your business.

Overhead expenses will range from 20 to 40 percent of income. For example, a weekend masonry job may give you $600 after paying for materials. Of that, $120 to $240 will go for equipment, tools, office expenses and taxes. The rest will be yours. Many part-time masonry services can earn an extra $15,000 to $30,000 a year working evenings and weekends. Some do even better.

How can I get started?

Masonry service is a trade. How much training and experience you will need depend on what type of work you do. A terrazzo mason may require 20 years of trade experience before starting a contracting business. A sidewalk installer may need only two years' experience.

Start gathering your tools. You will probably have many of them, but not the more expensive ones, such as mixers and tampers. You will also need the tools you will use in your office: a telephone, fax and maybe a computer.

If you're currently employed by a company as a mason, watch carefully for an opportunity to discuss your goals with your employer. Do so carefully, because some employers may consider you a potential competitor and fire you on the spot. Others will welcome a known subcontractor and help you get your start.

The SIC code for masonry services is 1741-01.

Mobile beautician

What will I be doing?

Not everyone can or wants to go to the beauty shop. Some customers of cosmetology prefer at-home or at-business service. Working from your own home, you can offer this service to your own group of customers.

A mobile beautician does about everything a shop beautician does: hair, facial, nails, other beauty services. The difference is *where*.

What will I need to start?

If you've graduated from a school of cosmetology or have a few years' experience in the beauty trade, you probably have what it takes to start your mobile beautician business: skills.

You will also need some equipment. What you need depends on what you do. Keep in mind that your equipment must be mobile. You can install a drying hood on a two-wheel dolly for portability. In addition, you can use cases for most of your equipment. Remember to use two smaller cases rather than one larger one if weight is a concern. You may want to limit yourself to customers in single-floor buildings or those with elevators.

Who will my customers be?

Your customers are asking for special service. Most will be willing to pay for the convenience of having you come to them. For example, elderly customers with restricted travel can be found in nursing homes or hospices. They would probably love to have someone come in and do their hair.

With a company's permission, one enterprising mobile beautician set up her shop in the women's rest room at a large factory. Appointments were made for the workers' lunch hours, which were staggered. Once a month, the beautician would set up during the dinner break for the swing shift.

How much should I charge?

The hourly rate for a mobile beautician is slightly higher than a shop beautician. You are offering convenience, as well as skill. A typical rate would be $35 to $75 an hour. Most beauticians will start at the lower end of this scale until they become busier than they want to be. Use your hourly rate to establish pricing by the specific job. A coloring may take one and a half hours. If so, quote your price for the session, rather than your hourly rate.

One mobile beautician simply multiplied the going rates for standard services by one and a quarter to two for the convenience factor and travel time. If a trim was $18 at a shop, she would charge $22.50 to $36 for the same trim at the customer's home or office.

How much will I make?

Once established, your billable time will approach 90 percent. The other 10 percent of your time will be spent on building business and keeping records. Depending on the cost of your equipment, 25 to 50 percent of your income will go to cover overhead expenses, including taxes.

How can I get started?

Begin keeping your eyes open for opportunities. One beautician offered her current employer a 10 percent fee for any customers they sent to her Sunday mobile beautician service. It worked out well for everyone.

Develop a flier that outlines your services, costs and how to make an appointment. Distribute it to friends, relatives, nursing homes, hospitals, professional offices and anyone else who may need a mobile beautician.

Musician

What will I be doing?

Nearly everyone enjoys music. If you're a musician, you can build a part-time business that's both profitable and fun.

A musician plays music to entertain others. Some musicians also teach music to others. Using professional shortcuts and books, even a mediocre musician can make a few bucks in an enjoyable trade.

What will I need to start?

It's surprising how many professional musicians don't read music. They've learned chords, progressions, riffs and techniques that make them sound nearly as good as classically trained musicians. To make the big time, you'll need lots of skills and talent. But to play a local club with a weekend band, you can probably learn what you need to know in just a few months.

You will, of course, need your chosen instrument and some skill at playing it. You'll also need some sheet music. Fortunately, how-to-fake and shortcut books containing popular songs are available, making them easier to learn and play. These books are available at most music stores.

Who will my customers be?

With basic music skills and lots of practice, you can hire yourself out as a musician for parties, night clubs, bars and taverns, and to individuals. You probably won't be able to get an agent, but you can book your own act at many smaller clubs. Consider joining other musicians in a group that plays and books together.

How much should I charge?

Musicians are frequently paid by the hour. A rate of $25 to $50 is common, but it will be split among all members of the group unless you're a solo musician. Some musicians specialize to develop a following and a higher hourly rate. Musicians sometimes work "on the hat." That is, they are only paid by the patrons as the musician passes the hat. It's no way to get rich, but it's easy to get hired.

How much will I make?

You won't be directly paid for setup or practice time. However, most of your other time will be billable. Overhead expenses, once you own your instrument, are minimal. You can use your personal telephone number as your booking number for a while. You'll need fliers and some business cards. And you'll have to pay taxes on what you earn. The rest is yours to keep.

A new musician can earn an extra $5,000 to $15,000 a year working part-time. To make more, develop your talent at playing music and at marketing your skills.

How can I get started?

Watch local newspapers for ads asking to book groups or to replace members. For example, "Wanted: Country bass player for three-piece band with weekend gig." If you haven't seen many ads, place your own: "Wanted: guitar/drummer looking for 3-piece country band for gig."

Some areas require union membership, so ask professional musicians you know about local unions. Union membership may get you on a hiring list or help you find an agent.

If nothing else, find a proven spot for a sidewalk musician and go to work. Play what you like and hope that others like it too.

Nail salon

What will I be doing?

A nail technician doesn't need much space in which to set up business. In fact, many nail technicians are independent businesses operating within beauticians' businesses. A nail service or nail salon does manicures, pedicures and related beauty services.

What will I need to start?

Some states require licensing, while others don't. Some training is typically needed. If you've attended beauty school or learned how to beautify nails, all you need is some manicuring tools and equipment. These can be purchased at beautician supply stores.

Who will my customers be?

Your customers are beauty shop customers who also want nail service. You can work by appointment or offer drop-in service. Many nail technicians work weekends, filling in time around appointments by asking beauty shop patrons if they would like nail service as well. To develop customers, some offer specials in conjunction with the beauty shop, or even a free trial. One enterprising salon offered "first hand free" to all beauty shop patrons. Nearly all saw the difference between the finished and unfinished hand and had the second one done—for a fee.

How much should I charge?

Nail salons typically charge $25 to $45 an hour, pricing services by the job. Check your competitors to determine what customers will pay them for manicures, pedicures and other services.

How much will I make?

Your income will be based on appointments. So your goal will be to get a follow-up appointment from every customer you can. By simply offering initial trial sessions, you can build your business.

The beauty shop will get 25 to 50 percent of your sales dollars, in exchange for rent, utilities, advertising and other promotion. The cost of your tools and supplies will be minimal, usually less than 10 percent of your income.

How can I get started?

Once you have the needed skills and equipment, contact beauty salons in your area to find out about renting a table, just as some beauticians rent a chair.

Next, develop your own flier with services and prices. Circulate it to friends, neighbors, beauty shop customers and other potential customers.

The SIC code for nail salons is 7231-02.

Newsletter publisher

What will I be doing?

Newsletters inform and promote. A newsletter publisher designs and produces a newsletter for business clients to distribute to their customers. Publishing a newsletter requires researching, writing, editing, producing and printing news documents for a target group.

What will I need to start?

To publish effective newsletters for others, you'll need writing, printing and promotional skills. Many of these skills can be developed as an employee of a newsletter service or in the promotions department of a large company.

As a newsletter publisher, you may design and write the newsletter, but leave production to a desktop publishing service. If you do your own production, you'll need a computer, a printer and desktop publishing software. You'll also need some training or experience using these tools.

Who will my customers be?

Most newsletters are published by and on behalf of businesses and business groups. Those done for smaller charities and individuals are produced by volunteers. You can volunteer to produce a newsletter to develop the skills you need for a paid newsletter publishing service.

Hospitals use newsletters to promote their services, with publicity written as news stories. Companies promote their products and services to customers and prospects with newsletters. Associations promote themselves and their members with newsletters. How much should I charge?

The hourly rate for newsletter publishing is $30 to $70, but most are priced by the issue or the page. For example, a newsletter publisher may research, write, produce and mail company newsletters for $500 to $1,000 per published page (plus printing and postage costs). That means the publisher is estimating 15 to 30 hours a published page at about $35 an hour.

How much will I make?

Marketing will take up 20 to 30 percent of your time, once your business is established. Overhead expenses will take 30 to 40 percent of what you make for computer, supplies, office expenses, taxes and other necessities.

How can I get started?

If you don't have a lot of credentials as a newsletter publisher, volunteer to produce them for one or two of your favorite charities or organizations. They will pay costs, while you donate your labor. If you do this, make sure you specify how long you are willing to make this donation. Depending on the group's budget, you may be able to ask a small fee for future work. Or you may have enough paid work to drop the training.

Contact the Newsletter Publishers Association (800-356-9302) for more information.

The SIC code for newsletter publishers is 2721-04.

Newspaper stringer

What will I be doing?

There are more than 18,000 newspapers in the U.S., most of them relying on full-time reporters and feature writers. However, for news on outlying areas, many newspapers use part-time freelance correspondents called "stringers."

As a newspaper stringer you will write local news stories and articles for one or more large newspapers. One successful stringer covers news on the Oregon coast for daily and weekly newspapers in other parts of the state.

What will I need to start?

To be a freelance stringer you must know how to write. You don't have to be a trained journalist, but you must know how news stories are written and what you can and cannot say. A friendly newspaper editor may help with the basics.

You will also need a way of delivering your fast-breaking stories. Some newspapers may prefer one method over another. The options are: mail, electronic mail (via Internet, CompuServe, America Online, etc.) or fax. Some newspapers will supply you with a fax or an online service, but would prefer that you have your own.

Who will my customers be?

Customers for your newspaper stringer service will be regional and metropolitan weekly and daily newspapers. For example, if you live in rural Iowa, you may string for a paper in the state capital (Des Moines), as well as in regional metropolitan areas (Minneapolis, Chicago, St. Louis) if something newsworthy happens nearby. Contact these papers now so you know who to call—and who they should call—if something big happens in your backyard.

How much should I charge?

The hourly rate for stringers varies, depending on your skills and your contacts. If you write a weekly column on happenings in Podunk, your rate will be $10 to $20 an hour, or even less. If you're covering a local disaster for many national newspapers, your rate will be more than $50 an hour.

Your pricing will often be established by the newspapers. Most papers pay by the column inch. That is, once the story is published, they measure the number of inches your story is and multiply it by their rate. A 10-column-inch-long story paid at $1.50 per column inch will earn you $15. Unfortunately, they don't care how much you wrote, they only pay for what they use.

As you develop skills and contacts, try to get a retainer or other fee from each paper you work with. For example, you will send the paper a list of hot local topics once a week for a regular fee. You are the paper's eyes and ears in the area. For the service, you get a fee. You also get paid for any stories you write.

How much will I make?

If you write stories "on spec" or speculation, you will be paid only for what is accepted. If you write "on assignment," you will be paid for everything you write. Of course, try to get everything on assignment. But as you start, you may have to write a few stories on spec.

As your stringer business grows, you may be able to get newspapers to pay your research expenses. They probably won't pay for your telephone and other overhead expenses (about 20 percent of your income), but they may give you money for gas and a meal or two when you're researching a story they've assigned.

How can I get started?

The best way to get started is to develop samples of your newspaper writing. You can write for small papers or cover big local stories for larger newspapers. Call editors to find out what papers need and pay.

Also look for local stories. If you know the local council meeting is going to be controversial, call newspaper editors to see if they will be covering it and, if not, if they will assign you to cover it.

Keep copies of all stories you sell, called "clippings," and show them to editors.

Contact state newspaper associations for a list of regional papers.

Packaging/shipping service

What will I be doing?

There are more than 10,000 full-time packaging and shipping services in the U.S. Is there room for those who want to offer this service part-time from their home? Certainly.

A packaging/shipping service prepares products for shipping or storage. Someone wants to ship Christmas or birthday presents to Uncle Harry in Peoria. You can gather and wrap them, select the best delivery method, contact the shipper and request pickup, and even track the package.

What will I need to start?

To offer services as a packager and shipping coordinator you must know a few things about each topic. Contact the U.S. Postal Service, United Parcel Service, FedEx and other shippers to learn their requirements. Some have weight limits and others have size limits. They will furnish you with information on preparing shipments, and even some tips on how to wrap and prepare packages for shipment.

Because your business will be operated from your home, it's important that your home be centrally located. That doesn't mean you must live at the edge of a six-lane highway. But you can't operate your business from atop Mt. Palomar. Shipping trucks may be able to get to you, but your customers won't.

Who will my customers be?

Customers for your packaging and shipping service will be individuals and small businesses. One customer may want to return goods to a manufacturer, while another needs to economically send a box of clothing to a third-world country. You must be ready for each.

How much should I charge?

Your hourly rate for packaging and shipping service will be $20 to $45, but you will price by size or weight or by percentage of shipping charges. For example, if you learn that it takes 12 minutes to package and label a 4-cubic-foot box and your hourly rate is $30, your time is 0.2 hours x $30 or $6. Add the price of packing materials and shipping charges for the total price.

You will sell packing materials at retail prices, set at about double the wholesale price. A box you buy wholesale at 78 cents will be sold to your customer at $1.56.

Shippers often add about 10 percent of shipping charges for their handling. So a box that costs $11.50 to ship will add a $1.15 handling charge.

If you can, get the pricing sheet from a competitor's packaging and shipping service to guide you in establishing your pricing.

How much will I make?

Most of your time will be billable, because the clock doesn't start until a package shows up. Until then, you're working for free. Overhead expenses range from 15 to 35 percent, depending on what equipment you need. An established packaging and shipping service can bring you $4,000 to $10,000 a year for part-time work.

If you prefer not to have customers and trucks coming to your home, you may want to set up a weekend shipping service at a local shopping mall or other central location. This, of course, will add to your overhead.

How can I get started?

Packaging is easily self-taught. Many shippers offer booklets and videos on how to pack for safe shipping. Also contact them to ask about establishing an account and gathering resources.

Consider who you will be offering your services to and how to best reach them. Many services develop a simple flier that they give to friends, neighbors, small businesses and others.

The SIC code for packaging and shipping services is 7389-88.

Personal consultant

What will I be doing?

Everybody needs some good advice. If people describe you as knowledgeable and helpful, consider becoming a paid personal consultant.

A personal consultant offers advice on physical and mental images. A personal consultant assists individual clients with wardrobe planning and personal shopping, and provides corporate clients with workshops and seminars on professional etiquette. People who want to look and feel better may hire you as a personal consultant.

What will I need to start?

You will be selling both knowledge and wisdom on a specific personal subject. You may be selling your ability to select clothing or help clients make good choices. In any case, you must have extensive knowledge and abilities in your chosen field. After all, you're an expert.

You must also be personable. Friendly advice sells better than unfriendly information. So you'll need patience, diplomacy and some psychology.

Who will my customers be?

Most of your customers, understandably, will be individuals. You will be offering them advice to help them live better. If you are an image consultant, your customers will be those who don't feel good about their image. Or your customers may be corporations who want to help employees project images of strength and competency.

You can also offer your personal consulting services to groups through seminars and classes that you design or that are established by local colleges.

How much should I charge?

Personal consultants earn an hourly rate of $30 to $70 or more. Well-known personal consultants who have written popular books on their topics earn much more.

Most personal consultants price their services by the value of the expected results. That is, a personal consultant who helps enhance the image of corporate executives will charge more than for a similar service to new college graduates.

How much will I make?

Many people will be reluctant to use your services unless they have heard many good things about you. This will require some time to develop your own image. Once established, you'll probably spend 20 to 30 percent of your time marketing your services.

Fortunately, overhead expenses for personal consultants are usually low. Advertising will be your largest expenditure. Otherwise, it's telephone, office supplies and taxes. Expect 20 to 40 percent in overhead expenses.

How can I get started?

First, become an expert in your field. If you consult on clothing or makeup, make sure you know as much as you can about these topics. Read, study, learn, try, ask.

Second, let others know you're an expert. If you have successfully consulted people, ask for letters of recommendation or other references. Write articles about your topic for newspapers or magazines and, if published, get copies out to potential customers.

Check area telephone books for other personal consultants and learn from them. Contact the Association of Image Consultants (800-383-8831) for more information.

The SIC code for personal consultants is 8742-03.

Personal fitness trainer

What will I be doing?

The fitness craze has been around for awhile, but it seems to have renewed interest. If you're into fitness and want to help others become fit, consider becoming a personal fitness trainer.

A personal fitness trainer helps clients set and achieve personal fitness goals. Most fitness trainers specialize in exercise, but they also help with diet and breaking bad habits.

You may work with people in your home, their home or in a gymnasium. Take your choice. Many personal fitness trainers meet their clients at a local gym. One trainer works with a group of six that meets in one section of a gym on Saturday mornings. Another trainer visits homes where customers have exercise equipment, to coach and encourage.

What will I need to start?

To train others in physical fitness, you must be a good example of the results. That doesn't mean you have to look like a body builder or a professional wrestler, but you do have to look and be healthy. You are your best advertisement.

To start, you'll need to know as much as you can about the why and how of physical fitness. Read the latest books and magazines. Find out what works best. Most important, learn how to motivate others toward good fitness habits.

Who will my customers be?

Your customers will usually be individuals who want to look and feel better. You can find them through advertisements in local newspapers, on gym bulletin boards and by circulating your brochures.

Sometimes you can contract with a company to help employees meet physical fitness goals individually and as a group. One company offered to donate $5 to charity for every pound employees lost during a specific month. They hired a personal fitness trainer to help and to track results.

How much should I charge?

Many personal fitness trainers establish an hourly rate of $35 to $75. Newer trainers may establish lower rates for the first six months. Trainers then may price services by the length and number of sessions or by the goal.

How much will I make?

About 20 percent of your time will be required to market your services, depending on your marketing skills, your credentials and your customers. Plan to spend more time marketing when you start your business.

Overhead will range from 10 to 40 percent, depending on whether you furnish equipment, rent a room or have other costs. Some trainers need an office, while others have prospects contact them through a gym.

How can I get started?

Contact gyms, dance studios and other commercial fitness businesses in your area to discuss your credentials and ideas. If you don't yet have credentials, join the American Fitness Association or a similar professional group and develop credentials.

Produce fliers that include your credentials, your programs, your prices and information on how to contact you. Give these brochures away anywhere and everywhere.

Personalized children's books

What will I be doing?

If you enjoy children and computers, consider publishing personalized children's books.

You'll be producing and marketing children's books that include a child's name and related information interwoven in the story. You may also sell related personalized products.

You don't have to write and illustrate the books yourself. There are many businesses that offer illustrated book pages you can personalize and print using a computer and laser printer.

What will I need to start?

The main ingredient to selling personalized children's books is a computer. You type in the child's name and other personal information that will be included in a specially written story starring the child. The results are sent to a printer, into which you've loaded the illustrated pages in their correct order. Print the pages and you have a book ready for instant binding on the spot.

Who will my customers be?

Most of your personalized children's books will be sold to grandparents, especially just before Christmas. Parents also buy these gifts, but usually around the child's birthday.

If you're selling personalized children's books year-round, consider mail order from your home. If your books are seasonal, rent a cart, kiosk or booth at a shopping mall.

How much should I charge?

The hourly rate for producing children's personalized books varies. If you produce books only when you have orders, your rate will be higher than if you have to sit in a mall waiting for customers. Excluding the waiting time, your rate should be $35 to $50 an hour for your time, your equipment and your overhead.

Most personalized books are priced at two to three times the cost of materials. An $11.95 book will wholesale at $4 to $6. Related personalized products will be priced in the same way.

How much will I make?

A retail personalized children's book publisher may make $500 one day and $50 the next day. The key is to find the best days and work them. Unfortunately, many shopping malls require all kiosk venders to be open all hours that the mall is open.

A mail order personalized children's book publisher will spend more time marketing and less time waiting. Marketing is more expensive than waiting, so costs are higher for a mail order venture. However, the resulting hourly rate will be higher, because less time is wasted.

During the Christmas season, an efficient personalized children's book publisher can earn a few thousand dollars. The key to success is finding a busy mall where traffic is high, but competition is low.

How can I get started?

Publishing and selling personalized children's books requires that you have a computer, a printer and some special software for the job. You can find ads for personalized children's book business opportunities in magazines like *Entrepreneur* and *Business Start-Up,* available at larger newsstands.

Pet-sitting and pet-walking

What will I be doing?

Pet-sitting and pet-walking are two related businesses you can run from your home. You can keep pets in your home when owners are at work or on vacation. You can take dogs on walks. You can spend a weekend at a customer's home caring for and feeding dogs, cats, gerbils, fish or other pets.

What will I need to start?

The skills required for pet-sitting and -walking are minimal. Most important, you must love animals. You must also know how to control them. You may have to teach some dogs basic obedience commands, in order to control them on your walks.

Little equipment is required for this business. A telephone is necessary for your customers to call you. Business cards or fliers are helpful in promoting your services. Some local regulations require that you clean up any byproducts an animal drops, which requires bags, gloves and tools.

Who will my customers be?

Most of your initial customers will be people you know or who live nearby. Pet owners usually don't let strangers watch their animals. In other cases, you will get customers by referral.

One way of developing new business is to contact local pet stores. A flier in their store can bring you an instant reference. Offering to send customers to the pet store may earn your flier a prominent display. Also consider placing a small service ad in a local newspaper. Tell people what you do and how to contact you. Save revealing your prices until they call you.

How much should I charge?

The hourly rate for pet-sitting and -walking depends on many factors, including where you're located. Your service may not find customers in a small town, but may do well in the downtown area or suburbs of a large city. The typical rates are $10 to $25 an hour, depending on number of pets and attention required. If you simultaneously walk six dogs for a half hour each evening, you can split your rate up six ways.

How much will I make?

Most of your time at this business will be billable and overhead costs are low, so you should be able to keep most of what you collect. This can make up for the lower rate. A part-time pet-sitting and -walking service can give you a couple hundred dollars a month doing something that's fun and easy.

How can I get started?

All you need to start this business is one customer. From a single satisfied customer you can find others by referral. One successful pet walker had a T-shirt with "Professional Dog Walker" and his phone number printed on the front and back. He gave business cards to anyone who seemed interested. Within a year, he was hiring others to walk dogs when he wasn't available.

Photography service

What will I be doing?

There are more than 20,000 full-time commercial photography services in the U.S. If you enjoy taking and/or developing pictures, this is an excellent home business that can offer income and satisfaction.

Commercial photographers produce and sell photographs of people, places, things. Some photographers specialize in portraits, while others photograph cars, pets or festivals. Other photographers look for unique subjects that are artistic or humorous.

What will I need to start?

You must have experience with cameras and other photo equipment, but you don't have to be an expert photographer to sell what you shoot. Many photographers go for quantity and select the best. If you shoot enough film, something's bound to come out well.

You'll need photo equipment, but you don't have to invest thousands of dollars into professional equipment. A good quality used camera can be purchased for less than $200. Professional photographers say that the most important tools they have besides the camera are lenses and lighting. Quality lenses and good lighting can make even a mediocre camera turn out quality photos.

Who will my customers be?

Who your customers are depends on what you're selling. If you take photos of beautiful scenery, magazine or calendar publishers may be your customers. If you photograph weddings, the wedding couple or their parents will be your customers. If you photograph products, the owner or manufacturer will buy your photos.

Once identified, you can find customers by thinking like them. If, for example, you wanted to find a photographer for a wedding, where would you look? You'd check the telephone book, ask friends, call wedding shops and watch the newspaper for ads. As a wedding photographer, those are the places you should be promoting your services.

How much should I charge?

Commercial photographers typically have an hourly rate of $35 to $75, but they price by the event or the value of the item photographed. You'll get more for photographing new or classic cars than you will for photos of traffic.

Wedding and portrait photographers, for example, design a package that includes commonly requested shots at a package price. It may include staging, makeup, lighting, photography, proofs and printing, but they are all offered for a total price. The photographer may also offer additional shots at a set price. This makes buying easier for the customer and assures profits for the photographer.

How much will I make?

How much time you spend marketing your photography service depends on what you're selling and to whom. For most businesses, plan on spending 20 to 30 percent of your time marketing your services.

Overhead expenses for a home-based photography service are lower than those for a retail business. Depending on how much equipment you need and its cost, plan on spending 25 to 50 percent of every dollar you get on overhead expenses. Simple photography using professional film-processing services requires lower overhead than buying expensive equipment for your own darkroom.

How can I get started?

The best way to get started in this business is by winning awards as an amateur photographer. Enter any legitimate contests you can, including showing your photographs at county fair judgings.

Produce a flier that tells others about your services and maybe even your pricing for standard packages. Finally, talk with editors of local newspapers to promote your new business.

The SIC code for commercial photography services is 7335-01.

Picture-framing service

What will I be doing?

Photos and drawings are enhanced by quality frames. If you enjoy working with art or with wood and other materials, consider a home-based picture-framing service. A picture-framing service designs, selects, constructs and installs frames on art, photographs and documents. It can be operated in or from your home, serving a wide variety of customers.

What will I need to start?

To start your picture-framing service you'll first need training or experience in selecting and constructing frames. You can get this experience working for a framing shop, studying books on framing and practicing with your own frames.

A framer typically works at a framing table with clamps, saws and other tools of the trade. For efficiency, you may need an air compressor to power a pneumatic stapler or other tool. Materials and supplies are available in wholesale framing catalogs and in stores located through most metropolitan telephone books.

Who will my customers be?

Customers for your picture-framing service include individuals, artists, other businesses and wholesalers. Some framers prefer to work directly with the public. In most areas, you have a choice.

One successful framer has four galleries as clients, all located in a resort town. She visits the shops once a week to pick up any art that requires a frame or frame repair and brings it back the next week. Another framer specializes in ornate frames for awards and certificates, selling his products to wholesalers.

Once you've defined who your customers are and what they want, it will be easier to find them through mailing lists and advertising.

How much should I charge?

Framing services typically establish a shop rate of $30 to $60 an hour, but price by the size of the frame, the complexity of the project and the quality of materials. A frame that requires 20 minutes to construct and install at $45 an hour means $15 in labor. Add materials at retail prices (two to three times wholesale) to establish the frame's price. Depending on clientele, you may be able to increase the price based on perceived value of the frame.

How much will I make?

Once established, your framing service will require about 20 to 30 percent of your time for marketing and administration. If you have few tools, your overhead will be about 25 percent of income, while a fully equipped shop may take up to 50 percent, including taxes.

How can I get started?

First, learn your trade. Develop knowledge and skills for framing by working in a frame shop or taking an adult education class on framing.

Next, create your own fliers and circulate them to potential customers. You can pass them out at art shows, at artist's club meetings and to friends and neighbors.

The SIC code for picture frame dealers is 5999-27 and 7699-15 for framing services.

Plant care service

What will I be doing?

If you have a love and a talent for taking care of plants, you can do so for others who will pay you. No, you won't get rich, but you can do a job that is rewarding on many levels.

A plant care service selects and cares for indoor and some outdoor plants for clients.

What will I need to start?

A plant care service sells knowledge and service. To start your home business you must know about and have experience with plants and plant care. If you don't already have one, you'll need a reference book on plants and their care.

You should be able to identify most house and outdoor plants by sight, as well as diagnose common plant diseases and problems.

Few tools are required for plant care, other than watering equipment. You will need a variety of plant foods.

Who will my customers be?

Many people who enjoy plants don't have the time or talent to care for them. That's where you come in. These potential customers are individuals, as well as managers of professional offices, retail businesses and meeting sites. Check your telephone book for potential competitors. If there are numerous plant care services in your area, consider specializing in a type or group of plants or clients. Otherwise, offer a variety of plant care services to the widest group of customers.

Let prospects know about your service by personal contact and small service advertisements in local newspapers.

How much should I charge?

The hourly rate for plant care depends on your skills and your ability to market. Many services establish prices based on hourly rates of $25 to $40. By working efficiently and minimizing travel, plant care services can competitively price by the visit, by the value of the plants or by special requirements. For example, a service may water and care for all plants in a suite of professional offices for $16 per office per month.

How much will I make?

Once you've developed a group of regular customers, you won't need to spend much time marketing your business. Until then, plan on spending up to half your time making contacts and building your venture.

Overhead expenses, including tools, supplies, office expenses and taxes, will take 15 to 35 percent of your income. The rest is yours. A successful plant care service can add $5,000 to $15,000 to your annual income once it's built.

How can I get started?

Learn all you can about plants and those who may want your help caring for them. If you specialize in caring for outdoor plants, look around to see who may need your service, such as office complexes or retail malls. Then carefully study the type of plants they have and what care they might need before approaching the owners to offer your services. Even if they have someone caring for plants, they may hire you as an adviser.

Develop your own flier that answers questions people may have about your service and its benefits to them. Some plant care services include pricing on the flier, while others don't. Look at what competitors are doing and do it better.

Pool-cleaning service

What will I be doing?

Anyone who has owned a pool or spa knows how much work they can be. They need to be checked and adjusted often. If you have experience caring for pool systems, consider a home-based pool-cleaning and maintenance service.

What will I need to start?

Equipment for cleaning pools and spas will vary, from floating cleaners to skimmers and chemicals. You will probably need a pickup truck or small van to carry your equipment and supplies from job to job.

Most important, you'll need training and experience with pool maintenance. While there are books and videos on the subject, nothing replaces hands-on experience. If this is a business you would enjoy, but you don't have enough training, consider working for a large pool maintenance service for a while to develop knowledge and skills.

Who will my customers be?

Most of your customers will be homeowners and apartment complex owners with private swimming pools. In some cities, pool owners can be found by checking the county tax assessor's records. You can also offer pool maintenance services to public pools or to gymnasiums.

You can try to find your customers through public records or you can advertise your services in local newspapers and let your customers find you. Most pool-cleaning services do both.

How much should I charge?

The hourly rate for pool cleaning and maintenance depends somewhat on equipment, services provided and the competition. However, many set prices based on an hourly rate of $30 to $50, then charge by the month or season. A weekly maintenance check and a monthly cleaning requiring a total of two hours can be priced at $60 to $100 a month, depending on your hourly rate.

How much will I make?

Pool cleaning and maintenance is typically done under a contract with the pool owner. This means that, once your contracts are written, you can concentrate on your work rather than on selling. Until then, plan to spend up to a third of your time marketing your business.

Your overhead expenses will range from 20 to 40 percent of income, depending on whether you supply chemicals or the customer does. In fact, some pool-cleaning services have two prices based on whether or not they furnish required chemicals. They may even sell extra chemicals to the pool owner, so additional profits are possible.

How can I get started?

Start by getting on-the-job training as an employee of a pool service, or at least by getting experience with your own or a neighbor's pool.

Let others know about your service by developing a flier that describes the benefits of what you do and why you are the best choice for pool service. Give prospects a reason to call you, such as a free pool checkup.

The SIC code for pool cleaning and maintenance is 7389-09.

Printing broker

What will I be doing?

Brokers bring buyers and sellers together. If you have experience in the printing trade, you may be able to work at home as a printing broker. A printing broker assists clients in purchasing printing services efficiently and economically. A broker also works with printers to find jobs for their presses. For example, in one day a broker may find a printer for 1,000 church booklets and then help a printer in Singapore find a new customer for their high-speed four-color press.

What will I need to start?

You must have a broad knowledge of the printing process and industry. You must also have contacts and resources within the industry. A broker must also be organized and detail oriented.

Your printing brokerage can operate from a room in your home with a telephone, answering machine and a fax machine. A computer is helpful, but not necessary. You'll probably want two telephone lines or call waiting service, so you can manage your calls.

Who will my customers be?

Your customers will be small businesses, manufacturers, publishing companies and printers. Some brokers specialize in one type of printing or customer, such as newspaper inserts or advertising agencies. Many brokers start small selling business cards, letterheads and envelopes to new businesses. Each printer supplies samples and a price list, from which the brokers get a discount. These brokers then move on to specialized printing as their knowledge grows.

You can find your customers by learning more about them and their printing needs. If you're selling business cards, for example, contact people who have filed for new business licenses in your area. The names will probably be available (for a small charge) through your state's corporation or business licensing office.

How much should I charge?

Printing brokers use hourly rates of $30 to $75 to help them establish pricing. The final price is typically in the form of a commission on the printing, ranging from 5 percent for large jobs to 25 percent or more for small jobs that require more effort per dollar spent.

Placing a $100,000 printing job may earn a commission of $5,000, while selling business starter sets (cards, letterheads, envelopes) at $200 each may earn $50 or more per set.

How much will I make?

At first, you'll spend at least half of your time selling your services and building a customer list. Then, as people begin coming to you, you will spend 10 to 20 percent of your time marketing and the rest getting paid for what you do.

Overhead expenses for a printing broker vary, depending on how much you rely on advertising and long-distance telephone services to conduct business. If you're working with local printers and customers, overhead may be as little as 10 percent of income. Most printing brokers, however, have overhead of 20 to 30 percent, including taxes.

How can I get started?

To start, set up an office in your home, create a brochure and business cards, and place advertisements in newspapers or magazines.

A printing broker must know the printing business and its resources. If you're inexperienced, you can teach yourself what you need to know about the printing trade. However, experience takes time. In the beginning, stick with small projects that allow you to get paid for developing your experience. Then keep your eyes open for bigger opportunities.

The SIC code for printing brokers is 2752-05.

Recycling service

What will I be doing?

Recycling has become big business. As much as 50 percent of materials in some automobiles comes from recycled materials. Other products, as well, depend on recycling materials. A small portion of these materials comes from consumer recycling bins. The majority is bought from services recycling for profit.

For example, one recycler was a man who stopped at furniture stores once a week to haul away the boxes dinettes and chairs were shipped in. He did the store a service at no charge, disassembling the boxes so they lay flat in the back of his pickup truck. Once he had a full load, he took it to a cardboard recycler in a nearby city, where he sold the load by weight.

What will I need to start?

To recycle for profit, you must know something about the needs of your resources and buyers. Many people will give you the materials in exchange for hauling them away. You will then need to know who wants to buy those materials from you.

You'll probably need some way of transporting what you recycle. Many recyclers use pickup trucks or open trailers pulled by cars. For smaller items, the trunk of a sedan may offer enough storage until your business gets off the ground. An enterprising recycler started his business by walking along rural roads as a self-appointed litter patrol, picking up cans and bottles that offered a return on deposit.

Who will my customers be?

Your customers will be wholesale recyclers. These are the folks who will buy your materials for recycling. You will get these materials from your resources.

To find wholesale recyclers, check area telephone books under recycling and related headings, depending on what you will be collecting. These may include cans, bottles, scrap metal, glass, paper, cardboard, plastics or all of the above.

How much should I charge?

You will be paid for your ability to find profitable materials for recycling. At first, your efforts to recycle may earn only $10 to $15 an hour. Once you've found materials in greater demand and a market for them, you should be able to earn $25 to $45 an hour.

With experience, you'll also get better at estimating material value, at negotiating and at knowing what current market value is. You may also find additional customers for your materials, giving you alternate places to sell.

How much will I make?

Your earnings may vary. How much you will make as a recycler depends much on what you know, what you do and for whom you do it. A new recycler may make only a few thousand extra dollars a year, while an experienced one can use weekends to turn an income of $15,000 to $30,000.

Overhead expenses directly relate to your costs to transport materials from your resources to your customers. If you already own a pickup or a car and open trailer, initial expenses will be small.

How can I get started?

The best way to start a recycling service is to learn what you can about it. Call recyclers in the telephone book. Check with municipal and state offices for government resources and guidelines. Ask people you know whether they have any resources or contacts.

Then, select customers to sell recycled materials to, find resources for these materials and start gathering them for recycling.

The SIC code for recycling services is 5093-12.

Referral service

What will I be doing?

People often need help finding someone to perform a service, and they find it handy to have a single source to call—a referral service. If you're one of those people others frequently call for advice, you may be able to offer your knowledge for money without leaving home.

A referral service finds, qualifies, selects and promotes businesses that meet specific business criteria or ethics. A referral service recommends and refers potential customers to businesses and associations for various services.

What will I need to start?

A referral service is paid for its knowledge and resources. The more knowledge and resources you have and the more valuable they are to your customers, the more you will be paid. The resources you offer depend on your specialty. For example, if you specialize in referring manufacturers to wholesalers, you'll obviously need a comprehensive source for wholesalers. These may be in the form of a little-known trade directory or your own research and experience.

Whatever type of referral service you start, you'll also need a telephone and a computer or typewriter.

Who will my customers be?

Referral services typically specialize in the needs of a specific group of customers. One may offer U.S. industrial contacts to foreign buyers. Another referral service may check out and refer travel services to corporate customers. A third service may help people new to a community find qualified doctors, dentists, attorneys, real estate offices and other professional services.

Once you've decided who your customers are, finding them will be much easier. For example, a service ad in a local newspaper can promote your handyman referral service. A brochure to restaurants can promote your service of finding and referring the best restaurant suppliers.

How much should I charge?

The hourly rate for referral services ranges from $25 to $50. Your pricing will be based on the time required to develop your referrals, but more on the value of these referrals to your customers. If your customers will save thousands of dollars by using your referrals, charging a few hundred dollars will be reasonable. If you're simply referring a plumber to a homeowner, your fee will be less because the value is less.

In some cases, the fee is paid for by the resource.

How much will I make?

Contacts will be everything in this business. Once you've developed qualified contacts in your field, most of your time will be spent on offering these resources to customers. About 20 percent of your time will be needed for promoting your services.

Expenses for a home-based referral service are typically 20 to 40 percent of income. This covers your office expenses, telephone and taxes. You get the rest.

How can I get started?

To start a referral service, pick a group of customers and a service you most enjoy working with. Then talk to people in this group to learn what they need and how you can help. Ask them what a good referral is worth to them. Remember to ask your resources if they would pay a finders fee for your referrals.

Finally, start small, help a customer or two and learn. When you've defined your market and services better, produce fliers you can circulate to potential customers.

Rental preparation

What will I be doing?

Moving into a dirty rental is frustrating. You can help people and get paid for it by preparing rental properties for occupancy. And you can do it with a home-based business.

A rental preparation service cleans and repairs rental apartments and stores for new tenants. Apartment preparation service, covered earlier in this book, is similar but not the same. Rental preparation services typically work for the new tenant, preparing the property so he or she can move in.

What will I need to start?

Your rental preparation service will need certain tools and skills, depending on what type of rentals you prepare. If you prepare apartments, you'll want portable cleaning tools that can easily be moved up and down stairs and elevators. Preparing homes for renters requires larger equipment that doesn't have to be as portable. Preparing commercial offices or retail stores may require even larger equipment, such as floor buffers or carpet cleaners.

Experience cleaning and preparing rentals will be important. If you have little experience, help friends or relatives who are moving or offer your services cheap to owners of new stores coming into your area.

Who will my customers be?

Your customers will be those who are renting or leasing residential or commercial property. You can find them by working with local real estate agents and leasing agents. One rental prep business started by making contact with a shopping mall's rental office. As stores left and new ones replaced them, the office told them about the prep service. The rental prep service also advertised in regional business publications.

How much should I charge?

The hourly rate for a rental preparation service varies, depending on what services are offered. Most services establish a rate of $25 to $35 an hour for cleaning and $35 to $60 an hour for repairs. Sometimes the repairs can be subcontracted to another home business, with a finders fee kept by the prep service. Estimate the work required to clean and/or repair a typical rental unit, then set your rate based on the square feet in the rental. Add a mileage fee to ensure that you are paid for your time and expenses to and from the job.

How much will I make?

Established rental prep services bill 70 to 80 percent of their time. The rest is spent on marketing and administration. Expenses eat up 15 to 45 percent of each dollar of income, depending on what services are offered, the equipment required and the efficiency of the owner.

How can I get started?

Most owners of rental preparation services have some experience cleaning and repairing homes, apartments or commercial space for themselves or others. This is valuable experience. If you don't have it, get it.

Next, find a need and fill it. Ask friends and neighbors about opportunities to help prepare rentals. You may be surprised how much initial business you can get this way.

Develop a promotional flier that tells what you do and how much you charge. Then get it into the hands of those who may need your services now or in the future, as well as those who work in the rental business. Contact real estate agents specializing in rentals and leases.

Research service

What will I be doing?

If friends and acquaintances have tough questions they need to research, do they come to you? Are you their personal reference librarian? If not, would you like to be?

A part-time research service can not only bring you extra income, it can also bring new information and fresh ideas into your life. A research service searches for answers to specific questions and information needs of clients. One client may need help researching a college term paper, while another needs to find out about a stock he is considering investing in.

Your job, should you choose to accept it, is to help them get valuable answers.

What will I need to start?

To start a research service you first need to have a love for research. You must enjoy looking at a question as a challenge, then finding the correct answer.

You will also need to know how to research efficiently. Someone will be paying you by the hour. There are many books available on advanced research techniques. Which ones are best? Research it!

You will also need access to research resources. This may require taking a class at a local university, so you can have access to the academic library. Or you may have the tools for researching online with your computer. Or you may live near a specialized research source that will give you access on your primary topic.

Who will my customers be?

Your customers are those who will financially benefit from the answer to a question you research for them. A small business would benefit from knowing more about a competitor or finding a new source of customers. A manufacturer would benefit from learning more about a technology that would benefit its business. A student would benefit from research you provide on a thesis topic. A homeowner would benefit by knowing what price similar homes in the area are sold for.

How much should I charge?

Your hourly rate depends on the value of the information you provide to your customer. A student will place less value on gathered information than will a business looking for cost-effective technology. The hourly rate will range from $40 to $125.

Once experienced, many research services can accurately estimate the time it will take to find the answer to a specific question. In this case, the service quotes a total price, taking into account the value of the answer to the customer. The price of preliminary research for a thesis paper may be priced at $250 while the same amount of research for a profit business may be priced at $750, because the value is different.

How much will I make?

Initially, your research service will require up to half your time for marketing. Once established, it will still take 25 to 40 percent of your time to find customers and gather resources. Overhead expenses are from 10 to 40 percent, depending on whether you're using a lending library or your own computer with an online service. Your expenses will also cover a telephone and some mileage. However, online database research costs should be added to your bill, because they can be quite high—from $35 to $250 an hour!

How can I get started?

First, learn as much as you can about the research process. Even if you are an experienced researcher, there are always new techniques and resources to discover. That's what makes this job fun.

Second, define your customers and their needs. What group do you feel most qualified to help? What questions do they typically need answered? Where should you go for these answers? How much time will this research usually take?

The SIC code for research services is 8732-06.

Resume writer

What will I be doing?

As a resume writer you will interview clients and write resumes and other employment documents for presentation to their potential employers. You must develop or have skills in interviewing people, as well as writing in commonly accepted resume styles and formats. You can work half-days, evenings, weekends or on-call, depending on your commitments and preferences.

There are about 7,000 full-time resume services in the U.S. with many thousands more operating part-time from home.

What will I need to start?

You can start a resume service with a telephone, an answering machine, a computer or typewriter, basic office supplies and a small advertisement in one or more local newspapers. You should also have reference books that include sample resumes for use as guides and for clients to select from. Quality papers and other supplies are available from local or mail-order stationery suppliers.

Who will my customers be?

Clients for your resume service are those needing help analyzing and communicating their marketable skills to employers. Because job seekers usually read the Help Wanted classified ads, advertising in area newspapers can draw many potential clients. Some resume writers interview clients over the telephone and mail completed resumes. Others interview face-to-face.

How much should I charge?

Resume writers typically offer standardized resume packages at set prices. The prices are based on stationery and printing costs, plus an hourly rate. Hourly rates for resume writers range from $30 to $50. You can enhance your income by offering additional products or services. Some services mail resumes for their clients. Others also sell booklets on job-seeking skills.

How much will I make?

A resume writer keeps about 40 to 50 percent of gross income as salary. A resume service operating 16 hours a week at an hourly rate of $35, and spending 25 percent of that time promoting the business, can earn $420 a week. A 40 to 50 percent salary offers an income of $168 to $210 per week. That's $10,000 a year for your part-time venture. Overhead costs (phone, stationery, printing, etc.) will take the rest.

How can I get started?

Contact the Professional Association of Resume Writers (3637 Fourth St. N., St. Petersburg, FL 33704; 800-822-7279) for membership information. PARW offers a certification program, marketing aids and a national convention.

Read *The Upstart Guide to Owning and Managing a Resume Service* by Dan Ramsey (Upstart Publishing).

Find and hire resume writers to prepare a resume for you. Analyze how you can improve on what they do as you start your own part-time resume service.

The SIC code for resume writing services is 7338-03.

Reunion planner

What will I be doing?

Everybody is curious about the whereabouts of their high school or college classmates. What are they doing now? What ever happened to so-and-so? Did our class president ever get out of prison? It's this curiosity that drives people to slim down, get a tan and attend their class reunion.

If you enjoy reunions, or at least enjoy organizing social events, consider planning reunions from your home. You don't even have to be a member of the group.

What will I need to start?

Planning a reunion requires organizational skills, some research skills, a few selling skills and a love for putting on a party.

If you have a computer, you'll need a database program for developing an address book of people to reunite. Otherwise, use file cards or address cards in a large Rolodex.

You'll also need people skills, as well as some negotiating skills for finding a meeting place and hiring caterers and entertainment.

Who will my customers be?

Your customers will be individuals who are or have been members of schools, churches, military groups or other institutions and who may want to renew friendships with others in the group.

How will you find your customers? Once you've identified what type of reunions you will specialize in planning, contact the organizations to learn what, if any, plans have been made for reunions. For example, call area high schools asking if any class reunions are being planned and, if so, who is coordinating them. If nothing is planned, ask how you could contact members to plan reunions.

How much should I charge?

It's difficult to set an hourly rate for reunion planning, because much of the work is detail. If you can standardize or automate your methods for efficiency, you can establish a rate of $30 to $60 an hour. Who pays? Each attendee will pay a cover charge for attending the event. You may also get a fee from suppliers, such as caterers, hotels or others, that benefit from your event.

How much will I make?

A class reunion of 200 people who each pay a $25 cover charge can bring you an income of $5,000. You will have catering or other expenses to pay from this, but your net income should be at least half of this amount. The cover charge will be smaller if your meeting is at a restaurant where people will order their own food off the menu.

Your overhead costs will go for research, mailings, telephone calls, advertising and taxes.

How can I get started?

The best way to start a reunion planning service is to volunteer to put one on for a group to which you belong. It can be a high school, college or trade school class, a military unit, a historical church or any other institution that draws people together. It can even be a reunion of employees lost in the big layoff of 10 years ago. Because you won't make anything from volunteering, you won't need liability insurance and you won't have to feel as bad if it doesn't go off smoothly.

Secretarial/word-processing service

What will I be doing?

Secretarial services perform professional office duties (typing, dictation, filing) for clients. In a typical day, a service may mail out 500 brochures, transcribe an accountant's dictation into letters and pick up a client's mail at the post office.

There are nearly 10,000 professional secretarial services in the U.S., with about half offering computerized word-processing services.

What will I need to start?

Your secretarial skills must be advanced and efficient. Your service may specialize in one or two skills, such as typing or dictation. If so, develop your skills and experience, earning certification if you can. You want your customers to have a reason to select your service over another.

Depending on the service you choose to provide, you may need a computer. One successful secretarial service is operated from home by a woman who produces and delivers documents electronically after her children are off to school. With her computer and online subscription, she can offer one day service while working her own hours.

Who will my customers be?

Most of your customers will be other businesses. They may be professional offices that have an overload of work or that have an employed staff lacking in certain skills. Once you've decided what kind of services you will offer, finding customers will be easier. If you specialize in medical transcription, contact medical offices in your area. If your specialty is legal dictation, try law offices. If you are adept at typing college papers, advertise where college students will learn about your services.

How much should I charge?

The hourly rate for secretarial and word-processing services ranges from $25 to $45. Depending on the services you offer and the type of client you serve, you may offer all services on a per-hour price. Other secretarial services price by the word, the page, the job or another method. A few are priced on retainer, furnishing a specific number of hours each week or month to clients under contract.

How much will I make?

Your established secretarial business will be able to bill at least 75 percent of your time to clients. The rest will be devoted to marketing and finding new customers. During the first few months, your service will require up to half of your time for marketing.

Overhead expenses for a secretarial and/or word-processing service depend on many factors, including what equipment you need to do your job. The typical range is 20 to 40 percent for overhead expenses, including taxes. That means you can probably keep 60 to 80 cents of every dollar you bring in.

How can I get started?

First, identify your potential customers and learn what secretarial services they will need.

Second, develop a flier that describes your services and their benefits, and invite the prospect's call for a free consultation or pricing. If your services are standardized, include your prices for these services.

Finally, get the word out. Let others know what you do and how you can help them. Ask friends, relatives former employers and business people you know for referrals.

The SIC code for secretarial services is 7338-05 and 7338-02 for word-processing services.

Security service

What will I be doing?

It's an insecure world. You can help people be more secure and feel more confident of their security by operating a security service.

A security service designs and manages security systems for individuals and businesses. One security service may install and monitor alarm systems, while another may provide bodyguard protection for rich or famous people. A third security service may help architects design buildings that minimize security problems.

What will I need to start?

To offer others security you must be an expert in your field. Once you decide on a field of expertise, develop your knowledge and experience in that field. If you want to offer a security guard service, for example, find employment in the field and get on-the-job training.

Some security services require knowledge of electronic equipment installation and use. You may sell and install burglar alarm systems in homes or stores. Or you may have an audio monitoring system in your home that allows you to listen in at homes when the owners are away.

In some fields of security you will need licensing and bonding. In others you may require training in electronics or in self-defense.

Who will my customers be?

That depends on what services you provide and who will most benefit. If you enjoy guarding valuable materials, offer a bonded guard service to businesses where crime has been a problem. If you specialize in designing and installing security systems, your customers will be those who have had break-ins in or near their homes or businesses. Reading police reports in the newspaper or at the police department will help you find your potential customers.

How much should I charge?

The rate for security services varies between $25 to $60 an hour depending on what services are offered and how specialized they are. Some security services price by the size of the system, while guard services typically charge by the shift, the week or the month. A security system can be priced based on the square footage of the area it secures.

Find out what your competitors charge in your area for similar services and you will have a starting point for pricing your services to be competitive.

How much will I make?

After a year of operation, your security business should be able to bill for 80 to 90 percent of available time. Overhead expenses will range from 20 to 50 percent, depending on whether you hire employees to do some of the work.

An established security system can net the owner $20,000 to $30,000 a year for a part-time venture.

How can I get started?

First, select a group of potential customers who have security problems. They may be people in a specific neighborhood, retail shopping district or industrial park.

Next, decide what products and services you can offer to make them more secure. It may be a patrol service, an alarm installation service, an alarm leasing service or a combination of services.

Finally, interview potential customers to learn how they feel about security, whether they have unmet needs and what they are now paying for security services or would be willing to pay.

The SIC code for security services is 7381-02.

Seminar service

What will I be doing?

People profit from learning. If you have knowledge that others can use, consider offering a seminar service. If you don't have the knowledge yourself, produce seminars that employ experts.

A seminar service designs, produces, coordinates and markets seminars on specific topics of value to others. If your expertise is in child care, for example, produce a short seminar for parents or for others who work in the profession. Or hire an expert to teach in a seminar you produce.

There are many good opportunities to teach and to learn with a seminar service.

What will I need to start?

To start a seminar service you first need to identify a group that will benefit from specific knowledge. It may be in a field where you are an expert or it may be in one that you have an interest. You then must organize the information and present it in a way that helps others retain it.

You will also need a meeting place. Some cities have popular seminar meeting sites, either in a convention center or at a popular hotel. Others hold seminars at schools or colleges. You'll need to identify and learn about renting such a site.

You will also need to reach potential customers of your seminars. This may be through newspaper advertisements and publicity or by contacting local business associations.

Who will my customers be?

Your customers will be those who will benefit from what you have to teach. In many cases, the greatest benefits are to those who financially profit from your knowledge, such as businesses or investors.

A professional writer may offer a seminar to would-be writers. A security consultant can offer seminars on improving home security or on alarm installation. An experienced truck driver may offer a seminar on how to drive to stay alive. Define your topic and your best customers.

How much should I charge?

Seminar fees are $35 to $80 an hour, priced by value of the seminar, time and competition. Of course, the cost is split among all attendees. For example, a seminar that requires 16 hours of preparation and 4 hours of teaching at $40 an hour has a cost of $800 (20 x $40). If split among 50 attendees, the price per attendee is $16. Add in snacks, room rental and a factor for no-shows, and your seminar fee is $30 per person.

How much will I make?

Most of your seminar service's time will be billable to one seminar or another. Overhead costs range from 15 to 45 percent, depending on whether you're including travel expenses and whether you need expensive advertising.

Some seminar services reduce costs by negotiating a percentage rental fee for the meeting site. A hotel may agree to free rental of a conference room, in exchange for 10 percent of the seminar fees. Another may offer the room free if you bring in 10 or more overnight guests.

How can I get started?

Learn from the successes of others. If you haven't already done so, attend various seminars in your area. Study how the seminars are organized and conducted. Estimate costs and income from fees to determine whether it is profitable. Decide how you would do it better.

Then try organizing your own seminar through local community colleges or adult education resources. The administrator may help you plan and market the seminar. Keep lots of notes. Learn from failures.

Sewing instructor

What will I be doing?

A sewing instructor helps others increase skills in sewing and related needlework crafts. Many sewing instructors conduct their own classes, with many students paying a few dollars each. Some teach commercial sewing skills or specialized skills.

You probably won't get rich as a sewing instructor, but if you love to sew and enjoy helping others learn, you'll find satisfaction in this part-time home business.

What will I need to start?

You don't have to be an expert seamstress to teach sewing to others. But you do need advanced skills and some experience teaching. You can practice teaching children or adult friends. You can teach free classes to develop experience and credentials. You can take an advanced sewing class and learn not only sewing techniques, but also teaching methods.

You probably already have the equipment and materials needed to teach sewing. If you will be teaching a group on sewing machine skills, you will need to find a classroom with enough machines. This may be in the home economics department of a large high school or a nearby college, or it may be in a sewing machine store's classroom.

Who will my customers be?

Your customers will be individuals and groups interested in crafts, especially for profit. The profit motive means that you will give your customers skills that they can, in turn, sell to others. You will be paid more for selling profitable skills than for selling recreational sewing skills. Sewing classes you can offer include how to make and sell aprons, teddy bears, puppets, historic clothing or other products for profit.

To find these customers and students, develop a flier on your classes and qualifications, then distribute it widely. Give copies to sewing centers, fabric stores, sewing club members and even small business development centers.

How much should I charge?

The hourly rate for sewing instruction is $25 to $40. Classes are priced by student and value. For example, a student in your class on sewing for profit will pay more than one in your recreational sewing class. The difference is value.

You may decide to offer your sewing instruction skills to a sewing machine center on an hourly basis, using their machines to promote their business. Or instead of an hourly rate, you may take half of the student fees for your time.

How much will I make?

Your successful sewing instruction business will require 10 to 20 percent of your time for marketing. Overhead expenses will range from 10 to 20 percent, unless you have to supply the students with sewing machines. Typical expenses include advertising costs, telephone, office supplies and some sewing materials. A part-time sewing instructor can earn an extra $10,000 a year, with eight hours a week at $30 an hour, less 20 percent overhead expenses.

How can I get started?

The first step toward your part-time sewing instruction business is to build your name and your skills. You can do both by offering introductory courses through local sewing machine stores, making sure your name is prominently displayed on all advertising by the store. Your fee will be smaller than if you conduct your own classes, but your expenses will be smaller as well. One successful sewing instructor teaches basic classes on an hourly rate, then offers advanced classes by renting the store's classroom.

Build your credentials by trying to get a feature story on your sewing skills in the local newspaper.

The SIC code for sewing instruction is 8249-05.

Shopping service

What will I be doing?

Some people hate to shop. They would rather spend time in the dentist's chair than in a mall. If you're *not* one of these people, but enjoy or at least tolerate shopping, consider a home-based shopping service.

A shopping service selects and purchases products and services for others. In some cases, customers are those who physically cannot go shopping. Others are those who dislike shopping. But most are those who simply don't have the time to shop.

What will I need to start?

To be a professional shopper you must be a smart consumer, knowing where to find anything without paying too much. For some clients, the price isn't as important as for others. They want a specific product for themselves or as a gift. So you must know where to buy nearly anything.

You must also be available to shop at a moment's notice. Depending on your client, you may have to drop everything to find an item the same day. Other clients won't be as demanding. If you cannot offer immediate service, develop your business with customers who won't require such service.

You will also need to establish accounts for your customers, unless they pay in advance. This can be a problem if your own credit cards are near their limits or nonexistent.

Who will my customers be?

Customers for your shopping service will be individuals, companies, hotels and groups. For example, a shopping service in New York City specializes in shopping for famous people who would be mobbed if they were seen in public. Another service shops for business gifts for a commercial real estate broker's clients. A third service shops for wholesale restaurant equipment for clients.

Identify what types of shopping you're best qualified to do. Then make a list of those who would most benefit from this shopping. Finally, consider how best to reach these potential customers.

How much should I charge?

Shopping services establish rates of $25 to $50 an hour, but often price their services based on the value of the purchased items with a minimum fee. The typical charge is 10 to 25 percent of the purchase, depending on the time and skill required, as well as the value of the purchased items. Buying $2,000 in business gifts may require just a few hours and a catalog. Buying Christmas gifts for friends and family of clients may take a few days.

How much will I make?

Repeat and referral business will expand your business once it is established. Until then, plan to spend as much as a third of your time marketing your shopping service. Overhead expenses are usually low (10 to 20 percent), because clients pay most expenses, including mileage, long distance telephone, postage and shipping.

A part-time shopping service can net $12,000 to $20,000 a year or more, depending on your clientele and your expertise.

How can I get started?

Some shopping services start by offering their skills as concierge to local hotels and convention centers. Keep your fee low and you will get more experience. Then ask for a letter of recommendation that you can use to promote your business.

Find a group of customers that you can serve well, do a good job for them and strive for quality personalized service.

The SIC code for shopping services is 7299-41.

Show promoter

What will I be doing?

If you enjoy promoting events, consider doing it for money from your home. A show promoter designs, coordinates, funds and markets events and shows for specific groups. You may bring a rock and roll revival to town or you may produce a local car show.

What will I need to start?

Show promotion is a craft. It requires attention to detail, promotional skills, a knowledge of the entertainment industry, contacts within the field being promoted (such as national booking agents), and an understanding of what shows will do best in the area.

You must have some proven experience in promotion. For example, you may have helped a local civic group put on a talent show or a special fund-raising event. You may have helped coordinate the arrival of an out-of-town speaker for your church.

To promote a show you will need to know who else promotes events in your area, as well as what media (radio, TV, newspapers) are typically used.

Who will my customers be?

Your customers will be those who pay admission or a fee to see an entertainer or speaker in your area. You may organize a local program for a touring musical group or a prominent personality, but your ultimate customers will be those who pay the bills.

You can find your customers by first identifying what types of shows you want to promote: business, entertainment, education, religion, etc. If your business tries to be all things to all people, it will probably serve none of them well enough to be profitable.

How much should I charge?

Show or event promoters earn a good income, with rates of $35 to $75 an hour. Most are paid by percentage of gate receipts or profits or by a set fee based on estimated time required to produce. For example, a promoter who produces a one-day seminar of business speakers may earn 10 percent of the admission fees plus 5 to 10 percent of the back-of-the-room sales of books and video tapes. A music show promoter's percent of gate receipts will probably be larger, but so will the risk of loss.

How much will I make?

Show promoters will build their business to a specific number of events per year or season. A music promoter may try to produce three or four shows during the summer or six during the year. A seminar promoter may work on just one or two sessions per year. Income from these events will range from $10,000 to $30,000 a year, after talent fees and overhead costs are paid.

How can I get started?

The best way to start is either to work for or follow the work of local show promoters, learning what you can from their successes and mistakes. You'll then be ready to try it on your own.

Small appliance repair

What will I be doing?

Do you enjoy tinkering with small appliances and other gadgets? Do people refer you to Mr. or Ms. Fix-It? If so, you may be able to build a successful home business repairing small appliances.

A small appliance repair service not only repairs but may resell toasters, microwaves, mixers and other household machines.

Fixing small appliances may not sound all that profitable, because many people simply throw away products that don't work. That's fortunate for the small appliance repair person who picks up these broken appliances for free or at a low cost, makes minor repairs on some and uses others for parts.

What will I need to start?

To start a small appliance repair service in your home, first learn how to repair appliances. My book, *Small Appliance Repair Made Easy* (Consumer Guide), will help get you started with troubleshooting techniques and lots of illustrations.

You'll need a few tools, but you may already have many of them: a voltammeter, soldering iron, pliers, screwdrivers, etc. Set up a workbench in your garage or a spare room and start collecting needed tools.

Who will my customers be?

Your customers will be small appliance owners who would rather fix than toss. Service advertisements in local newspapers and shopping guides will earn you your first customers. Stress the economy and ecology of fixing small appliances that don't work rather than buying new ones.

One successful small appliance repair service used a classified ad like this: "Wanted: broken small appliances." Those who called were told the advantages of fixing rather than discarding these appliances. If this wasn't successful, the repair person offered $2 for the appliance for parts. In many cases, the needed repair could be made in a half hour and the appliance resold.

How much should I charge?

The hourly rate for efficient small appliance repair is $25 to $50, with the lower rate for low cost appliances (toasters) and the higher rate for more expensive ones (microwaves). Once you've learned how to quickly diagnose small appliance problems, you can establish flat-rate pricing that is both economical for the customer and profitable for you.

How much will I make?

A small appliance repair service can bring in an extra few hundred dollars of income each month. Some services do better by using extra time to rebuild and resell appliances through local consignment stores. Others specialize in one or more related types of small appliances. The more you specialize the more you can charge, but the less business will be available to you.

Most small appliance repair services charge an hourly rate plus parts, so your overhead expenses won't include replacement parts. It will include the costs of your shop, your equipment, your telephone, books on repair and office supplies.

How can I get started?

If you don't already have experience in repairing small appliances, get it before you try to charge for it. Ask friends and neighbors for small appliances they are considering throwing away. Fix them and give them back or resell them as appropriate. Learn from each appliance you repair. Start building up your small appliance repair shop with a work area and needed tools.

Produce a flier that tells others what you do and what you charge. Place an ad in a local paper promoting your business.

The SIC code for small appliance repair is 7629-01.

Tailor

What will I be doing?

There are about 12,000 full-time tailors in the U.S. and many thousands more who work part-time from their home.

A tailor makes, alters and enhances clothing for others. If you have these skills and the experience, consider starting your own part-time tailor service.

What will I need to start?

Besides skills in alterations and clothing making, tailors also need to know how to work with customers. One tailor specializes in helping executives. She goes to the executive's office for the fitting and, once done, delivers the custom-tailored clothing to the office.

If you have experience in this trade, you probably already have the tools you'll need. Many tailors have a second set of basic tools they use on the road.

Who will my customers be?

Customers for your tailor service include individuals, clothing resellers and alteration shops. You can specialize in suits, for example, and offer your services to alteration shops that may not have anyone on staff who is as experienced.

How much should I charge?

The typical rate for tailors is $25 to $60 an hour, depending on skills, experience and name value. Many tailors price by service or by a percent of garment value. The percent will depend on the complexity of the garment and the skills needed for the tailoring.

Alterations will earn a lower rate, while clothing design earns a higher fee.

How much will I make?

An established tailor will spend just 10 to 20 percent of his or her time marketing the business. Fortunately, overhead expenses are lower than many businesses, ranging from 10 to 25 percent. Being able to work from your home gives you an advantage over tailor shops that must pay rent on a retail store.

How can I get started?

Contact local clothiers and alteration shops, letting them know of your experience and your rates. Some may already have a tailor, but may need to call another one for rush jobs or overload work. Give them your business card and flier.

Find ways to publicize your business in local newspapers and other media. If you have tailored clothing for the rich and famous or for people in another country, turn this interesting information into a feature story that can help you build local credentials and get you noticed.

The SIC code for tailors is 5699-19.

Teaching your special skills

What will I be doing?

Everyone has special skills that others need. For example, you may have skills dealing with children, elderly parents, bill collectors or pets. You may be good at tole painting, grading coins, fixing tricycles or troubleshooting appliances. You may be fluent in Farsi, knowledgeable about classic cars or informative on Iguanas. If you have knowledge on any specific topic, you can sell your expertise to others. The more valuable the knowledge is to others, the greater you will be paid.

What will I need to start?

You probably have most of what you need to teach your special skills to others: knowledge on a specific subject. Of course, you will also need teaching skills. Depending on what you teach, you may need other resources or equipment. For example, to teach others the skill of grading coins for collecting (numismatics), you'll need samples, some coin grading books and a magnifier.

Who will my customers be?

Customers for your skill-teaching business will be those who want or need your particular skills. Customers will be individuals, groups, schools, colleges, businesses and other organizations.

For example, if you're fluent in Farsi, your students will be those who want or need to learn this Arabic language. Some people *want* to learn it, but businesses may *need* to do so to trade in the Middle East. So your customers may be importers, exporters and business employees who deal in international trade. Is there a business magazine or newspaper in your area where you can advertise your training?

How much should I charge?

The hourly rate for teaching skills ranges from $20 to $75. You will price your training sessions by the class or by the value of instruction. So a class on Farsi (customer needs) will earn you more than a class on grading coins (customer wants).

For example, a class for businesspeople may have 20 students paying $25 each. If it takes you eight hours to prepare and two hours to teach your class and your income is $500 (20 x $25), your hourly rate is $50 ($500 ÷ 10 hours). Deducting 25 percent for overhead expenses (advertising, telephone, room rental), your net hourly rate is $37.50.

How much will I make?

Depending on how many classes you teach and how much preparation you require, your annual income can be $15,000 to $30,000 from this business. Overhead expenses will range from 10 to 30 percent or more.

How can I get started?

First, know your topic. Learn everything you can about your chosen subject. Take related classes taught by others. Develop your credentials.

Second, find customers. Who will most benefit from what you teach? How much will they benefit? What will your knowledge be worth to them?

Third, set your pricing, based on both cost and value. You will get more for teaching skills that, in turn, are profitable to your students.

Finally, tell others about your business. Develop and distribute a flier that describes your teaching topic and how it can benefit students. Set up a class or two and enroll students.

Telephone survey service

What will I be doing?

It's the call that everyone hates: the telephone survey at dinner time. But the people on the other end of the telephone provide a valuable service and can do so with friendliness and sensitivity.

They can also make money from home.

If you'd like to bring your energy and enthusiasm to a business that sorely needs it, consider operating a telephone survey service. Find an approach that encourages trust and conversation. Treat each caller like a person and your exceptional results will profit you in many ways.

What will I need to start?

To conduct telephone surveys you must know how to graciously get information from other people. You need to know how to politely probe. You may follow a prewritten script. If allowed, you may be able to vary how you ask a question for improved results.

You'll also need a telephone, of course, and an answering system if you expect return calls. If you are on the telephone much, invest in a head set (about $100) that prevents tired arms and neck.

Depending on what type of surveying you do, you may need a computer and related software. One successful telephone survey service conducts post-travel interviews for a tour company, asking how the customer enjoyed the trip and what can be improved. She works at a computer that handles all dialing and gives her a place to write the responses. Once a day, her reports are electronically mailed to her supervisor in another city.

Who will my customers be?

Customers for your home-based telephone survey service include small companies that market to individuals or other companies. Businesses want to know who will buy certain things or what they have bought. You can specialize in inquiry follow-up or did-you-buy calls that are placed a month after people request information about your customer's product or service. Or you may specialize in market research surveys that try to learn what people want from specific products.

Your customers will be businesses, advertising agencies, inquiry management services, fund-raising organizations and others who need to know what their prospects or customers are thinking.

How much should I charge?

The rate for telephone survey varies from $30 to $75 an hour, priced by value of information, the call or other measurables. One service charges by the number of responses gained in surveys. Another charges per call, whether the person completes the survey or not.

How much will I make?

Most of your time at this job will be billable to a client and overhead expenses are low. If you are good at your job, you can make a net income of $12 to $25 an hour after expenses. The more valuable the information you gather is to someone, the more you will be paid.

How can I get started?

Some people start this business by working for a phone shop, a business that has dozens of people making telemarketing calls from a big room. Unfortunately, they soon pick up bad habits, such as speaking to a telephone rather than a person and watching the clock. You may get better training by teaching yourself the needed skills at your own pace: Volunteer to make survey calls for the American Red Cross or another well-respected group. You'll learn as much without the pressure.

Once your experience is developed, contact local businesses to tell them what you can do for them: You can call their customers and prospects to get valuable information that will help the business grow and profit. Few businesses can afford to turn down a conversation with customers.

Temporary help agency

What will I be doing?

One of the best ways of developing skills for your home business is to hire yourself out as a temporary worker in your chosen field. You will quickly get on-the-job training, without the obligations of a long-term job. You may also meet some of your prospective customers for your own home-based temporary help agency. Such a service finds temporary laborers, office workers and sales people for business, industry and individuals. In many areas, temporary help agencies specialize in domestic, day-labor, crafts, office or other workers.

What will I need to start?

To start your temporary help service you will, obviously, need some temporary help. You will need to match jobs with qualified workers. In most cases, you'll gather workers through your advertisements and jobs through ads and outbound calls to employers. You'll need a telephone and a card file system or computer to track all your resources.

There are more than 16,000 temporary help agencies in the U.S. Competition in terms of quantity is high, but competition for quality is never very high. So be ready to offer quality service.

Who will my customers be?

Your customers will be retail businesses, manufacturers, service businesses and individuals—who all have a job to be done but don't want to hire a full-time person to do it. To minimize bookkeeping, the employers prefer to pay a fee to a temporary help service who will find a qualified worker, make sure he or she is at the job, and takes care of pay and taxes.

Who hires temporary help? An office may need a replacement for a vacationing secretary, for example. A warehouse may need workers to help unload a big shipment coming in the next day. A homeowner may need a temporary domestic helper for the holidays.

How much should I charge?

Temporary help services usually hire employees directly, as needed, paying taxes and sometimes benefits, and then collect a higher fee from the employer. For example, a laborer may be hired by the service for $8 an hour to unload trucks for a couple of days. The agency may get $16 an hour for the laborer's time, passing on half of it to the laborer and keeping the rest. After expenses, the agency may get a quarter of the fee, or about $4 an hour. To make money, the agency must have a number of workers out on jobs at any given time.

How much will I make?

You can make a little or a lot, depending on how efficient you are at finding and matching jobs and workers. You can work a couple of hours finding jobs and a couple finding workers for those jobs. Four hours of work a day can give you a weekly income of $500 or more. Or not. If not, look for jobs or workers that are easier to find and coordinate.

Your overhead costs, excluding payroll and taxes, will range from 25 to 50 percent of your portion of the pay. If you have five workers out at $12 an hour each and you pay them $6 an hour each, you're making $30 an hour. Your overhead will take up a quarter to a half of your portion after taxes are paid.

How can I get started?

Many temporary help services are begun by those who have experience as temporary workers. They know how the local market works, who needs temps and where to find them. They also know the importance of good service. If you don't have experience as a temp, become one for a while to learn the business from the other side.

Once you're ready to go into business for yourself, select a field of labor, contact temp employers and start lining up temporary employees. Develop business cards and fliers to help you promote your business.

The SIC code for temporary help agencies is 7363-04.

Tour guide

What will I be doing?

Many people love to travel and learn about new places. If travelers come to your area looking for fun and entertainment, consider being a home-based tour guide.

A tour guide organizes, markets and conducts tours. As a tour guide, you will help travelers see and learn about your area. Your tour guide service may specialize in international tours, camping tours, factory tours, historic tours, student tours or one of many other specialties. Because you work part-time from your home, your expenses will be low. And because you will typically conduct tours for groups rather than individuals, your hourly rate will be higher.

What will I need to start?

To help others get the most from their travel time, you need to be knowledgeable and efficient. You also need to understand travelers. It helps if you've traveled, because you will then empathize with your customers.

To start, decide what will be interesting to travelers coming to your area. It may be the sand dunes or a historic battlefield. Learn about them. Also learn about side trips that can make your tour better than anyone else's.

You may need a portable public address system, a mode of transportation or other tools, but you can probably rent or hire them for your tours.

Who will my customers be?

Customers of your tour guidance will be national and regional tour producers or individuals traveling on their own. One tour guide specializes in fishing expeditions on a famous nearby lake. Another offers insider tours of art museums that include special tours of areas normally not seen by the public.

Once you've decided who your best customers will be, it's much easier to contact them. The lake tour guide places ads in sporting publications. The art museum tour guide does the same in art and travel magazines.

You can also subcontract your guidance to tour operators. If so, talk with travel agents in your area about this opportunity.

How much should I charge?

The hourly rate for tour guides is $25 to $70. The more people have paid to get to your location, the more they will probably pay for a tour. Visitors from a neighboring county probably won't order your deluxe tour. Save it for those coming from a foreign country.

Tours will be priced by the number of individuals in the tour group. Rather than quote prices here, I suggest that you contact other tour services in your area and specialty for competitive pricing.

How much will I make?

A tour guide spends up to 40 percent of his or her time marketing. This time is not billable, but is included in the hourly rate. As your tour becomes better known, you'll spend less time selling it and more time giving it.

Excluding transportation costs, overhead expenses (telephone, office, taxes) will eat up 15 to 35 percent of your income. It will be 50 percent or more if you provide the transportation as well.

How can I get started?

First, get to know the travel business. Develop experience in the travel industry or as a traveler—or both. This will give you a valuable prospective on what travelers want and don't want in a tour guide service.

Second, study one or two unique tours you can offer with the least overhead expense. Learn as much as you can. Then design and offer a quality tour from what you've learned, promoting it to your selected group of customers.

The SIC code for tour guides is 4725-01.

Transcription service

What will I be doing?

If you take dictation, type like the wind and know technical terms, you can offer a transcription service from your home. A transcription service translates spoken words into written ones for medical, legal, editorial and other employers.

Some transcription services go a step further, summarizing transcripts for easier reading.

What will I need to start?

A transcription service today requires a computer with a word processor. It also requires transcription equipment, such as a Dictaphone, used by your clients. Some prefer small cassettes. In any case, you'll need equipment to listen and transcribe.

You will also need to know the language. Medical and legal terms are like foreign languages to those unfamiliar with them. You must know these words and how to spell them if you will be transcribing them. Fortunately, there are books and even computer software programs that will help. There are also courses you can take to help learn these terms.

Who will my customers be?

Your customers will be doctors, lawyers, editors and other professionals who prefer to dictate than to write their words. Most do it for efficiency or convenience. For example, you may transcribe an attorney's recorded notes into a contract or a to-do list. You may transcribe a doctor's recorded comments into a medical record. Or you may transcribe an interview between a writer and a famous celebrity for an upcoming book.

How much should I charge?

Transcription services establish a rate of $25 to $60 an hour, but price by the line, page or document. The price may be $1 a page or $30 for a client report. To price by units, select the typical unit for your field, estimate the average time to transcribe and process, then price it accordingly.

How much will I make?

Your established transcription service will probably require less than 20 percent of your time for marketing. Until then, you may spend as much as half of your time selling your service to others.

Overhead expenses depend on the equipment you need and your travel time, if any, between jobs. If all dictation is delivered to you, your overhead will be lower than if you have to travel to your client's location. Expect overhead expenses ranging from 20 to 40 percent.

How can I get started?

Build your skills. You will be paid for efficiency and accuracy. If you work slowly or make mistakes, you will lose business. Make sure you have the needed skills before you start your transcription service.

Contact potential customers, interviewing them about their transcription needs. What services would they like that they're not getting now? Define and promote your business. Focus on a specific type of transcription and customer, then go after it.

The SIC code for transcription services is 7389-17.

Translation service

What will I be doing?

Are you fluent in a language other than English? Can you translate or interpret for others? If so, you may be able to offer a profitable translation service from your home.

A translation service interprets documents and conversations between users of two or more languages. It also translates correspondence, newspapers, magazines and other materials.

What will I need to start?

Most translation services specialize in two or more languages, such as English and French—one that their customer knows and one that he or she doesn't. Some services specialize in a group of related languages, such as Asian. Others are proficient in the native American languages.

So you must have proficiency in at least two languages. You may prefer to translate written or spoken words. A literary translator can usually work at home in his or her spare time, while a vocal translator may be required to be on call for conference telephone calls or even travel.

You will probably need some tools and equipment to help you, such as language dictionaries and tapes and current books in the second language, to keep you informed on idioms and events.

Who will my customers be?

Your customers will be international companies, individuals, students and publishers. For example, an international manufacturer may want you to translate their product literature into a foreign language to help sell their products. Or a buyer may be visiting a foreign country and require vocal translation services while meeting with the manufacturer. Individuals may need letters from relatives in the old country to be translated. Foreign students studying in nearby colleges may need help with English. Publishers may need books to be translated into English before publication.

In most cases, letting others know of your skills and experience with foreign languages will draw business to you. However, you will need to make the effort to inform others through business cards, fliers and telephone calls. Customers won't automatically knock on your door unless they *know* you have something they want.

How much should I charge?

A translation service sets a rate of $30 to $75 an hour, depending on proficiency, type of translation and whether travel is required. A translator of books at home will typically earn less than a vocal translator who must travel to customer sites. The travel time won't be paid at the full rate, but the translator should be compensated for the extra efforts of travel.

Translation services price by the hour, the page, the class, the publication's length or other factors.

How much will I make?

Your experienced translation service will bill 80 to 90 percent of your time, with the rest spent on marketing and administration. To get your business off the ground, you may need to spend as much as half your time promoting your business and even do volunteer translation to develop credentials and references.

Overhead expenses for translation services include a telephone, office supplies, reference materials and taxes. Expect overhead costs of 10 to 30 percent for a home-based translation service.

How can I get started?

First, make sure you are proficient in the foreign language or languages you will be translating. Second, make sure you are proficient in English. If English is your second language, study the language formally and also listen to native speakers for idioms. To translate well you must know at least *two* languages well.

Third, get the word out. Let others know about your skills and service. Depending on the language and type of translation you prefer, contact businesses, importers, exporters, students, publishers and others who need to cross language barriers.

Yes, even translation services have an SIC code: 7389-20.

Tree-trimming service

What will I be doing?

A tree-trimming service does just what the name implies: trims trees. Tree trimmers are called to remove limbs or trees that are diseased or damaged. They also remove limbs close to power, cable and telephone lines. They are called to remove trees that have fallen onto a house or into a road.

Their service is important and their income is good.

What will I need to start?

To offer a tree-trimming service, obviously, you must know something about trees, how they grow and how to remove them or stop growth. Experience is also important.

Your equipment will include a chain saw, tree saws, cutters, trimmers and related equipment, as well as ladders and maybe a climbing belt. You will also need to wear goggles, a safety hat and other safety gear.

Who will my customers be?

Customers for your tree-trimming service are easy to find. Simply drive through neighborhoods and business districts, looking for trees that need tending to, then contact the landowners. One trimmer took Polaroid photos of problem trees and brought them to the owners with suggestions on how to take care of them. In many cases, the solutions sounded like too much work to the owners and the trimmer was hired.

Wind storms can play havoc on trees and limbs. Listen to regional news and if a wind storm hits a neighboring area, get there fast. Offer your services to area tree trimmers, insurance agents, disaster relief offices or individual homeowners. (Stop by city hall first and make sure you have the proper licenses for the area.)

How much should I charge?

Tree-trimming services set rates of $35 to $60 an hour in most areas, depending on equipment, efficiency and competition. If all you have is a ladder and a saw, your rate will be on the lower end of the scale. A pickup truck with a "cherry picker" hydraulic bucket and power saws will get the higher rates.

To fill in time between emergency jobs and driving through neighborhoods, offer tree maintenance services. Once a month, you can check and trim trees for apartment or business complex owners. Your fee will be slightly lower than standard, because you will have annual contracts that guarantee some income. How you charge for this service depends on what you do.

How much will I make?

A tree-trimming service can give you $10,000 to $30,000 in spare-time income each year. Deducting overhead expenses of 25 to 50 percent for advertising, telephone, equipment, office supplies and the inevitable taxes, gives you a good part-time income.

How can I get started?

Learn as much as you can about trees and how to efficiently maintain them. Community colleges and universities with agriculture departments can direct you to courses and books on these subjects.

To gain experience and to discover the best tools and techniques for the job, practice on your own trees or offer to trim trees for friends, neighbors, churches and others. Even better, work part- or full-time for a tree-trimming or landscaping service. The experience you gain will help make you more money later.

Let others know about your services and their benefits. Produce a flier with pricing. Order and distribute business cards. Talk with others about trees and how to maintain them. Let people know you're an expert.

The SIC code for tree-trimming services is 0783-01.

Tutoring service

What will I be doing?

A tutoring service helps others, often remedial or advanced students, learn additional facts or skills about a subject. If you are knowledgeable on a topic, you can make it more enjoyable—or at least easier—for others to learn by being a tutor. Or, you can help people find qualified tutors.

What will I need to start?

To teach a subject you must first make sure you have extensive knowledge on the topic. You don't necessarily have to be an expert, but you must at least know more than your students. You must also know how to transfer that knowledge.

Practical experience may help to make the subject come alive for students. For example, in teaching physics, conducting experiments can help students visualize concepts and learn faster than reading from books. So, depending on your subject, you may need lab equipment.

In some states, tutors must be certified and licensed. Check with area colleges on requirements for tutors in your state.

Who will my customers be?

In most cases your customers will be college students or the parents of high school students. You can reach the students or parents through advertising and brochures. Referrals from teachers are also very useful.

How much should I charge?

The hourly rate for tutors depends on the topic, complexity of the material, credentials and teaching skills. As a successful tutor you will be able to establish a higher rate than new tutors. Typical rates are $25 to $50 an hour, with most tutors on the lower end of the scale. If a tutor is teaching graduate-level quantum physics, for example, he or she is likely to command the higher rate.

Some tutor services offer package deals, such as on-call tutoring as needed, priced by course. For example, a chemistry tutor will help a student throughout the course whenever a question arises or to prepare for an upcoming test, for a flat fee of $200 per course.

One enterprising tutor located in the midwestern U.S. has a toll-free number and charges services by the hour to students' credit cards.

How much will I make?

About 80 percent of your time will be billable once your business is established. Overhead expenses for reference materials, telephone, office supplies and some advertising will range from 20 to 40 percent. A tutor working eight billable hours a week at $30 an hour with 25 percent overhead will net $180 a week or nearly $10,000 a year. There are many college students who pay their tuition by working as tutors in their strong subjects.

How can I get started?

If you have little or no experience as a tutor, develop your skills by volunteering to tutor others on your primary subjects. Develop your resources. If one or two textbooks are most popular in your field, buy them or borrow them from students you're tutoring.

Ask for referrals. If you're in college, ask teachers and professors if they would recommend you to other students. Also ask your students for referrals. Produce a flier on your skills and include your telephone number or other way to contact you. Include references or testimonials.

The SIC code for tutors and tutoring services is 8299-09.

Used car sales

What will I be doing?

There are more than 77,000 full-time used car dealers in the U.S. Many thousands more supplement their income buying and selling used cars from their home. To reduce expenses, some dealers also take cars on consignment—selling cars for other people and collecting commissions.

Why would someone buy a used car from a private party or home-based dealer? Mainly for reasons of trust. Used car lots typically get their cars from regional wholesalers who, in turn, get them from other dealers. Many of these cars are questionable units that dealers don't want to sell themselves. A small home-based used car dealer can pick and choose, buying directly from car owners. Car buyers often prefer to purchase from friends or from other people they feel they can trust.

What will I need to start?

To start a car dealer business from home you'll probably need a license. Contact your state's department of motor vehicles for requirements. Many say that you need a license and a bond if you buy and sell more than a few cars in a year. Don't ignore the law; comply with it.

Of course, you'll need cars. You may decide to buy and sell them yourself or you might prefer to sell them for someone else on consignment. You can find cars by placing ads in local newspapers and shopper guides. An ad might be worded, "I buy used cars for cash." If you can't come to terms with a caller on a profitable price, offer to take the car on consignment.

Who will my customers be?

Your customers will be individuals buying cars. You may also sell cars to other dealers in your area. To find customers, advertise specific cars in local publications, including auto trader magazines.

One home-based auto dealer specialized in classic British sports cars, such as MGs, Jaguars and Morgans. He soon developed a following, as people came to know him as the "British sports car guy." He typically had only one or two cars for sale, but he knew where to find dozens more if customers showed interest. He was also a member of a regional sports car club that brought him in contact with other enthusiasts and car buyers.

How much should I charge?

Although a used car dealer can establish an hourly rate of $25 to $45, most do better pricing by value of car and typical profit potential. For example, the wholesale value of a car may be $1,100 and the retail value $2,300. Buying the car at $1,100 and selling it for a negotiated price of $1,900 nets the dealer $800 in gross profit. Many part-time used car dealers set a goal of selling one or two cars a month.

How much will I make?

With advertising costs your greatest expense, overhead for your used car business will typically be 10 to 25 percent of your gross profit. In the example above, the gross profit is $800. Net profit will be $600 to $720. Overhead expenses should include $50 to $150 per car for detailing or cleaning up the car for sales. Some cars need more work than others.

How can I get started?

Don't try to compete with local used car lots. Instead, be friendly competitors and help each other. Specialize. Sell four-wheel drive units, pickup trucks, family sedans, ugly ducklings, vanity cars, classics or some other type of car that others aren't selling.

Learn how to advertise. Advertising is your biggest expense (beside the cars), so advertising smart can make the difference between a profitable business and a hobby.

Make sure your business won't interfere with the rights of your neighbors to a quiet neighborhood. Minimize traffic by displaying cars and meeting buyers and sellers elsewhere, if necessary.

The SIC code for used car sales is 5511-03.

Valet-parking service

What will I be doing?

Are you looking for an easy weekend business that doesn't require any cash to start, yet can pay well? Consider a valet-parking service.

Used by restaurants, hotels, night clubs and people having parties or weddings, a valet-parking service parks cars, performs security and delivers cars to owners.

What will I need to start?

For a valet-parking service you will need good driving habits, honesty and a willingness to serve others well. A clean shirt or blouse also helps.

You may require bonding or insurance to sell your services. Talk with your insurance agent to learn who insures your driving and parking—you, your customers or the cars' owners.

Who will my customers be?

Your potential customers will be restaurants, hotels, night clubs, event planners and even car rental agencies, which sometimes need cars delivered to important clients.

How much should I charge?

A new valet-parking service may earn $20 an hour, while one with a prime location and efficient service can earn $40 or more. The service is typically priced by the car, the hour or the event. In better locations, valet services work for tips only.

How much will I make?

If you plan your service to coincide with busy times, it will be profitable. If you have to stand and wait for customers, you will lose money—unless you receive a minimum hourly fee from business owners. Overhead expenses are practically nil, except for taxes and some business cards. You may also need an insurance policy or bonding.

A wedding with 100 cars parked at $3 a car (paid by the event planner) will give you $300 for just a few hours' work. However, this much activity may require one or two assistants to share the work load. You can pay them a commission, by the hour or by tips only.

How can I get started?

To start a valet-parking service, offer your skills free of charge to churches or chapels conducting weddings. Parking for tips will give you strong motivation for efficient and friendly service. Visit busy upscale restaurants to watch how they efficiently valet cars. You'll learn fast. Then you'll be ready to move on to more lucrative customers.

Video-copying service

What will I be doing?

A video-copying service is the perfect home business for someone who understands how to make VCRs work.

Actually, there's more to it than that. A video-copying service transfers film, photos or other video to video. It may also add, mix or copy sound to tape. What services you provide depends on what customers need, what competitors are already doing well and what skills and equipment you have.

A video-copying service does not duplicate copyrighted materials for resale. That's pirating and is punishable by the FBI. Instead, a video-copying service transfers customers' old 8mm home movies, still photographs, keepsake videos and other images to one or more video cassettes.

What will I need to start?

Depending on what services you offer, you'll need at least two quality VCRs and a TV for viewing. You may also need a video transfer box, sold at electronic stores for less than $200, to transfer 8mm, slides and photo prints to video. Of course, to transfer from film you'll also need a projector.

You'll need a source for quality video tapes at wholesale prices. Initially, you can buy them at discount stores. But you will soon need cheaper sources, which can be found through regional telephone books.

You'll need some experience, as well. The operating manuals for your VCRs will get you started. In addition, look for books on video recording and transfer at libraries and bookstores.

Who will my customers be?

Customers for your video-copying service will include individuals, companies and groups. For example, a wedding photographer may need 12 copies of his video for customers. A company may need 100 copies of a training video it produced. A family may want old home movies and photos transferred to video for an upcoming reunion.

Study your local marketplace by checking the telephone book and visiting camera shops to learn what video-copying services are now available, and look for a need that you can fill.

How much should I charge?

Video copying typically earns an hourly rate of $30 to $45, depending on what's being done. That doesn't include time spent waiting for videos to copy. The hourly rate includes setup time and actual work time.

Video copying or duplication is often priced by the hourly rate, the length, the complexity of service or the value of the resulting tapes. As an example, making copies of a customer's tape may require 10 minutes of setup time per tape at $30 an hour. Thus, each tape requires $5 in labor. Add in the retail price of the tape (which you bought at wholesale), and you have your basic price.

How much will I make?

The income of a video-copying service depends on many factors, including the speed of the copying equipment. Professional duplication equipment, costing a thousand dollars or more, can simultaneously make multiple copies in a fraction of the time used by consumer VCRs.

A video-copying service that duplicates for wedding photographers, for example, can copy numerous tapes over a weekend, earning a gross income of $100 to $200 or more a week with basic equipment. Overhead expenses vary, but will range from 10 to 30 percent of income, excluding blank tapes.

How can I get started?

The best way to start this business is to offer video copying services to friends and family for the cost of the tapes, assuming you already have or can borrow the equipment. Learn about tapes, equipment, customer needs, pricing and marketing opportunities. Then offer your services to larger clients and use contracts to fund professional video duplication equipment. Don't buy much beyond what you need, but keep your options open for expansion.

Research this business opportunity by reading video magazines, talking to dealers, finding equipment catalogs and talking with potential customers.

The SIC code for video-copying services is 7819-02.

Wallpaper service

What will I be doing?

One of my friends loves to wallpaper. She sees every painted wall as a challenge. She knows what papers look best in a room and, most important, how to apply them. If this describes you as well, consider offering a wallpaper service based from your home.

A wallpaper service selects, prepares, installs, trims and removes printed wallpaper. Some wallpaper services contract directly to paint and paper stores, while others work with remodeling contractors or directly with the public.

What will I need to start?

Hanging wallpaper, as anyone who has tried knows, requires skill. Doing it fast and well is a craft. To start a professional wallpaper service you'll need to first develop your skill and craft.

You will also need to know how to select the most appropriate wallpaper for a room, or to advise your customer how to do so. This requires some design training and experience. Many decorating books cover this topic adequately and can be purchased at bookstores or found in public libraries.

Equipment needed for hanging wallpaper is minimal. A ladder, a work surface (counter, card table, portable work bench), a tray, brushes, rollers and seamers are all that's needed for most jobs. If you also remove wallpaper, buy removal tools, such as a heat gun or steamer and putty knives. You will also need tools for preparing painted walls for wallpaper.

Who will my customers be?

Customers for a wallpaper service include individuals, companies, interior decorators, contractors and retailers. Most services start with individuals and build the business and reputation, then move on to contractors. Others who have contacts in the contracting industry start there.

How much should I charge?

A wallpaper service establishes prices based on a rate of $30 to $70 an hour. Quoted prices are based on the square foot and complexity. For example, a 120-square-foot (10 x 12) room that requires three hours to prepare and paper at $40 an hour may be priced at $1 a square foot. If priced by the wall surface, the same room with 300 square feet of wall surface can be priced at 40 cents a square foot. The cost of wallpaper is added to this amount, due to the wide variation in prices and quality.

How much will I make?

A part-time wallpaper service that can finish a room an evening, five nights a week can earn a gross income of $400 to $700 a week. Deduct 20 to 35 percent for overhead expenses and your net income is $260 to $630 a week, or about $13,000 to $32,000 a year. Of course, you must be very efficient at both installation and marketing, but it can be done.

How can I get started?

First, learn your trade. Develop your skills selecting and hanging wallpaper for yourself and others. If you do it for others at no charge, ask for a letter of recommendation and referrals when you're done.

As available, take classes from wallpaper manufacturers and decorating courses at community colleges.

Develop business cards and a flier that tells about your services, pricing and references. Then distribute these marketing tools to individuals, interior decorators, paint and wallpaper stores, remodeling contractors and others. Also include a small advertisement in the services section of your local newspaper.

Contact the Guild of Professional Paperhangers (513-222-9252) for more information.

The SIC code for wallpaper services is 1721-04.

Wedding planner

What will I be doing?

A wedding planner or consultant plans, budgets, arranges and co-ordinates weddings and related events. A wedding planner helps take the stress out of these emotional events.

The U.S. has more than 8,000 full-time wedding consultants, with thousands more working part-time from their home.

What will I need to start?

To be a wedding planner you must first be an efficient planner. You must be able to coordinate many tasks at once, handling both people and things with confidence and skill.

The greatest tool in a wedding planner's business is his or her notebook. In the notebook are the names and data on prospects, clients, wedding resources and other information that make the difference in the success of wedding events.

Who will my customers be?

Your customers are obvious: engaged couples and their relatives. What may not be as obvious is how to reach these potential customers. Local bridal fairs are a good source of leads if you can buy lists of the attendees or, better, have booths there. Also, develop friendships with wedding suppliers who can refer your services, such as photographers, churches, flower shops, cake decorators, etc.

How much should I charge?

Your hourly rate as a wedding planner will be $25 to $50. You will use this rate to establish a flat fee per event or a percentage of the wedding budget. Flat fees for planning a wedding range from $500 to $2,000 for the wedding event and reception. Other planners price on a percentage of the total event budget, typically 10 to 20 percent. Wedding suppliers (caterers, musicians, equipment rental) are paid separately.

How much will I make?

Your new wedding planning service will require as much as 30 percent of your time for marketing and promotion. Once established, about 10 percent of your time will probably be enough to keep your business moving at a profitable pace. Of course, this depends on your marketing skills, competition and referrals.

Overhead expenses for a wedding planner usually range from 15 to 30 percent after suppliers are paid. So a wedding that grosses $1,000 in income will net you $700 to $850 and probably require 15 to 25 hours to plan and manage.

How can I get started?

You may already have experience planning and coordinating wedding events. If not, start volunteering to do so for friends or relatives, asking for a letter of recommendation from them when the event is successfully done.

The SIC code for wedding consultants is 7299-32.

Window-cleaning service

What will I be doing?

Cleaning windows is certainly not a glamour job, but it can be a profitable part-time home business.

A window-cleaning service is hired to clean glass and other smooth surfaces. Some services work only at ground level—no ladders. Others specialize in cleaning windows at heights. It's your choice, but remember, the less competition the greater the income.

What will I need to start?

The main key to success as a window cleaner is efficiency. An efficient window cleaner knows what products work best, how to use them and how to clean efficiently. A wholesale janitorial service in your area can suggest products that other services use. They may also be able to help you select equipment, and even find your first cleaning jobs.

Who will my customers be?

Your customers will be retail businesses, managers of offices and municipal buildings and individuals, depending on what opportunities are locally available. In a small town, your window-cleaning service may do all types of windows. In a large city you may specialize in ground-level retail stores in a specific part of town.

Once identified, finding prospective customers is much easier. Contact them individually or develop fliers and mail them to prospects. If you don't quite know who you want to serve, offer your services to all types of customers. You'll soon learn whether you prefer to work with homeowners or businesses.

How much should I charge?

Window-cleaning services establish rates of $25 to $55 an hour, pricing services by the job or by the month. For example, cleaning windows on a 1,500-square-foot home, you discover, takes you about two and a half hours. With a $30-an-hour rate, that's $75. You can price the same home at 5 cents a square foot (.05 x 1,500 = 75). Or if there are 12 windows, you can price the job at $6.25 a window. Your efficiency and customers' needs will dictate your prices. Competition will also help you set prices, because you don't want to charge much more than others who do the same job.

How much will I make?

About 25 percent of your time will be spent marketing your business, except during the first month or two when half of your time will go to finding customers. Once established, 15 to 35 percent of your income will be needed to pay overhead expenses including basic equipment and cleaning supplies.

How can I get started?

Many window-cleaning service owners learn the trade by working for others. You can find jobs cleaning windows for janitorial services or window-cleaning services. Develop your skills and your knowledge. Then, once you work efficiently and have some contacts in the business, consider offering window cleaning services on your day off or evenings.

The SIC code for window-cleaning services is 7349-04.

Woodworker

What will I be doing?

If you enjoy making things with wood, consider turning your hobby into a part-time business as a woodworker.

A woodworker designs, makes, finishes and markets products made of wood and related materials. Woodworkers can easily work and sell from home.

What will I need to start?

The key to success as a woodworker is craftsmanship. You must know your trade. If you have experience as a professional or hobby woodworker, you may already have the needed skills. If not, start now on getting them.

You'll also need tools. Which tools depends on what wood products you will be making. You may choose to carve wooden figures or make coffee tables or kitchen cabinets. The tools for each job are different.

You'll also need a source of materials at prices that offer you a profit. You may be able to establish a wholesale or contractor's account through a local lumber retailer or a national mail-order supplier, found through trade magazines.

Who will my customers be?

Your customers will be decided by what you make and how you sell it. For example, if you sell small wooden craft items at flea markets, your customers will be individuals who visit your booths. If you carve decoys, your customers may be individuals, retailers or even wholesalers.

To reach your potential customers, learn as much about them as you can. What do they want? How much are they willing to pay? Where do they shop for these products? Who are your competitors? Become a customer for your product, so you can learn how the customer buys.

How much should I charge?

The shop rate for woodworkers varies from $35 to $75 an hour. Newer woodworkers with few tools may earn less, especially during the first year of operation. Most products are priced by the estimated time and materials in them, with an added factor of value. That is, if a product costs you $11 to produce and market, but you know that people will buy it for $20, price it at $20.

For more specific information on pricing woodworking, read my book, *The Woodworker's Guide to Pricing Your Work* (Betterway Books), available through most bookstores.

How much will I make?

Woodworking is a production business that requires 20 to 30 percent of your time for marketing. If you produce in quantity for wholesalers, your marketing time will be less than if you sell to individuals at flea markets.

Your overhead costs will range from 25 to 50 percent of your income, depending on production costs.

How can I get started?

Learn your trade. Find woodworking products that you enjoy making and that people need or want to buy. Learn as much as you can about the marketing and pricing side of your trade, because it can make the difference in your profitability.

The SIC code for woodworkers is 1751-06.

Writer

What will I be doing?

A writer gathers and translates information, ideas and emotions for others. A writer may write advertising copy for brochures, how-to articles for magazines, novels for book publishers, technical manuals for industry or other literary products.

What will I need to start?

Writing is a craft. As a craft it can be taught and learned. Although John Steinbeck was an artist at writing, he was also a craftsman. You may never become a Steinbeck, but you can learn enough about the craft of writing to sell your work.

You'll need a computer to become very efficient at writing. My first articles were written on an old manual typewriter. But today I would not consider writing without at least a basic computer and word processing program, because they let the writer revise without retyping. And revision is the key to good writing.

Who will my customers be?

Your customers as a writer will be book, magazine, newspaper and newsletter publishers, advertising agencies, marketing services, businesses and manufacturers, depending on what you write about and for whom. As a numismatist, you may write about coin collecting for readers of coin magazines. If you have technical knowledge, you can write about it, translating and simplifying information into instruction manuals. As a parent, you can write about your experiences and offer tips for magazine readers.

How much should I charge?

Your hourly rate as a part-time writer will be $20 to $75, depending on your writing and marketing skills. In most cases, you will be paid by the published word or by a percentage of a book's retail or wholesale price. By-the-word rates range from 5 cents to $1 or more per word. Book royalties are usually 5 to 15 percent of the book's retail price, with some publishers offering an advance of a few thousand dollars to keep you happy until the royalties start coming in.

How much will I make?

Marketing is as important to a writer's success as writing skills. So plan to spend 25 to 40 percent of your available writing time on marketing your ideas to publishers and businesses. Overhead expenses range from 20 to 45 percent of income and include office supplies, reference sources, research costs, telephone, postage and taxes.

How can I get started?

Writing is a learnable craft, so start learning. Subscribe to writer's magazines. Consider enrolling in Writer's Digest School or taking an evening course in writing to learn your craft. There are also numerous books on the craft of writing available at bookstores and libraries. *Writer's Market* is a particularly good resource. Study other people's writing and learn how to define and develop a topic. Specialize in a field and in a type of document. For example, if you have parenting skills, write articles for a variety of magazines. If your full-time job is as an auto mechanic, write articles that help readers solve automotive problems.

Writers, too, have an SIC code: 8999-03.

Appendix

Worksheets
for weekend
entrepreneurs

Opportunity Worksheet
What will I be doing?

To help you select and evaluate weekend home business opportunities in this book, first answer these questions:

What would I like to be doing (output)?

_____

_____

_____

What would I need (inputs) to produce these outputs?

_____

_____

_____

What business experience I had?

_____

_____

_____

What challenges or limitations do I have?

_____

_____

_____

What time is or will soon be available to me?

Daytime:_____

Evenings:_____

Weekends:_____

Seasonal:_____

Other:_____

What hours or days do I prefer to devote to a part-time business?

_____

_____

_____

Resource Worksheet
What will I need to start?

To help you start weekend home business opportunities in this book, first answer these questions:

What knowledge or training do I have?

_____

_____

_____

_____

_____

What skills have I developed?

_____

_____

_____

_____

_____

What financial resources do I have?

_____

_____

_____

_____

What tools and equipment do I have or can easily get?

_____

_____

_____

_____

What other resources are available to me?

_____

_____

_____

_____

Customer Worksheet
Who will my customers be?

To help you find customers for your weekend home business, answer these questions:

What products or services have I been a customer for?

_____

_____

_____

_____

What have I learned about being a customer?

_____

_____

_____

What do I know about the needs of these potential customers?

     Individuals:_____

     Groups: _____

     Professionals:_____

     Retail businesses:_____

     Wholesalers:_____

     Manufacturers:_____

     Governments:_____

     Schools:_____

Where would I first look for customers?

_____

_____

_____

What would be my motto or attitude toward my customers?

_____

_____

_____

_____

Price Analysis Worksheet
How much should I charge?

To help you price products and services for your weekend home business, answer these:

What hourly rate is typical for selected businesses?

_____

_____

_____

What are the primary products and services I would offer?

_____

_____

_____

_____

How much time does each product or service require to produce?

_____

_____

_____

What supplies or materials does questions each product or service require to produce?

_____

_____

_____

_____

What unit does each product or service use for pricing (session, job, page, etc.)?

_____

_____

_____

How do my potential competitors price these products or services?

_____

_____

_____

Income and Expense Worksheet
How much will I make?

To help you figure profits from your weekend home business, answer these questions:

What will my hourly rate probably be?

_____

_____

About how much of my business time will be billable?

_____

_____

_____

What and how much will my overhead (office supplies, telephone, etc.) expenses be?

_____

_____

_____

_____

_____

What and how much will my variable expenses (materials, etc.) be?

_____

_____

_____

_____

_____

How much will typically be left over as my salary and profit?

_____

_____

_____

How much will I take out as a salary or reinvest into the business?

_____

_____

Income Reporter

Date	Cash/Check	For	From	Amount

Expense Reporter

Date	Cash/Check	For	To	Amount

Cash Flow Reporter

DATE:

FOR TIME PERIOD:

	Date:		Date:		Date:	
INCOME	ESTIMATE	ACTUAL	ESTIMATE	ACTUAL	ESTIMATE	ACTUAL
Opening Balance						
TOTAL INCOME						
EXPENSES						
TOTAL EXPENSES						
Ending Balance						
Less Minimum Balance						
CASH AVAILABLE						

NOTES:

Inventory Reporter

Location:

Item#	Quantity	Description	Price	Total

TOTAL

Priced By:

Checked By:

Invoice

Invoice:	P.O. #:	Date:	Sales Rep:

Sold to:	Ship to:

Qty.	Description	Price	Total

Notes:

Subtotal	
Sales Tax	
Total	

Index